Screen, Page, and Place

I0422257

Over three decades of writing on films,

books, and travel

Richard T. Owen

PublishNation
www.publishnation.co.uk

In memory of my mother, Glenys Mary Owen (1926-2015)
who taught me a love of words, both written and spoken.

About the author

Richard Owen was born in Porthmadog, Gwynedd in 1953. He graduated in 1978 with a doctorate in pharmacology and has worked for several pharmaceutical companies including Wellcome and AstraZeneca. Since retiring, he has published over thirty reviews on drugs in a peer-reviewed journal. Although a scientist, he has a keen interest in cinema, books, and travel and has written about these subjects in various magazines and university and corporate newspapers. He is the author of *The Apothecary of Joy and Other Stories*, a collection of short stories, published in 2016.

CONTENTS

Introduction

We are all critics now—Twitter, Facebook, Instagram, TripAdvisor, Trustpilot, Amazon, blogs, and vlogs entice or pester us to provide instant or anonymous opinions, images, and rebuttals. Whether locally, nationally, or globally, it all happens at breakneck speed. It wasn't always thus. In the pre-digital age we relied on newspapers, magazines, radio, and television for informed opinions about the arts and travel. As a child of the pre-digital age, my jottings on films, books, and travel were all conducted via the medium of old-fashioned print. My university and two of the companies I worked for produced weekly or monthly papers or magazines through which I poured my random thoughts on this film, that book, or that place.

My opinions may or may not chime with yours and on reflection, I'm not sure that even I now hold the same thoughts on some films or books. It matters not—criticism is not a science and is subject to change with time. What matters is that you have your own opinion, but I'm grateful, as Alexander Walker puts it in his book, *It's Only a Movie, Ingrid*, for the '*pleasure of bearing witness*'.

FILMS

'Of all the arts, the cinema is the most important to us.'

Vladimir Ilyich Lenin

(1870–1924)

If Lenin was alive today, he would no doubt substitute the word cinema with social media.

Lenin considered cinema important for propaganda, agitation, and education. Today, social media has overtaken some of these functions, notably propaganda and agitation. Whether social media can be construed as belonging to the 'arts' is a moot point. Sites devoted to film criticism such as RottenTomatoes.com allow audience reviews to sit alongside those from published critics. A quick glance allows you to see the percentage of all critics, top critics, or audience members who gave the film a positive rating. Reducing a film's rating to 'positive' or 'negative' or 'fresh' or 'rotten', as in the Rotten Tomatoes site, sadly eliminates nuance, subtlety, and ambiguity.

As Caspar Salmon states in his *Guardian* article entitled 'Who needs film critics? Actually, we all do': *'the best film criticism is an art that can help unfold beauty ... [it can] ... reveal new facets of a film ... [or] ... cause your thinking to depart on a new tack. The critics may not be the first to the film and there is usually a discrepancy between critical consensus and audience opinion.'* Social media often tries to amend the professional critical viewpoint. Filmgoers have a wide range of online options to gauge a film's quality but embracing the views of a range of the best critics, prospectively and retrospectively, can add to their pleasure in ways that mere audience reviews cannot. If critics disappeared, advertising would then become the main channel for disseminating information on film.

Reviews from *Javelin, Tabloid,* and *Respect* (1975-1998)

Javelin was the newspaper of the University of Bradford which I attended from 1971–1978. It was only during my PhD period, 1975–1978, that I wrote film and book reviews for *Javelin*. Nobody asked me to do so, I merely put my first review under the editor's door and was astonished to see it appear in the next edition of the paper. I carried on with these 'surreptitious mailings' and it was only some three months later that I actually met the then editor, Phil Wharton. Phil was an accomplished musician and composer and scored many of the university's plays, including *The Master and Margarita* which won a Fringe First Award at the Edinburgh Fringe Festival in 1977.

On re-reading these reviews I've noticed a tendency to name drop quite extensively, namely the 'back room' contributors one never sees, cinematographers, designers, etc. Whilst this may seem very pretentious, it was my way of recognising that whilst the actors' work may only be on the screen intermittently, the work of e.g. the designer, composer, or cinematographer is on screen *all the time*, whether the actors were there or not. If I saw something that pleased my eye, an impressive set for example, I wanted to know who to praise, who was responsible. Conversely, and this rarely happened, it gave me a slightly perverse pleasure to name the guilty party if I thought the work below par. Not that it mattered—since no one within the film industry would read my reviews anyway (as far as I'm aware!) but it would be too late for any corrections even if they had. *Tabloid* was the newspaper of The Wellcome Foundation Ltd and *Respect* was the internal magazine of Zeneca. I discuss these briefly before the relevant sections.

The information in square brackets and italics before or after some reviews includes information which was added after their publication, e.g. Oscar or BAFTA wins, or other trivia. I have occasionally, but not routinely, included nominations for Oscars or BAFTAs.

Film Reviews

1975

Rollerball
(Dir.: Norman Jewison)

In a corporate-controlled future, an ultra-violent sport known as Rollerball represents the world, and one of its powerful athletes (Jonathan E. played by James Caan) is out to defy those who want him out of the game. The posters inform us that when wars no longer exist, there will still be Rollerball. Quite, but one could almost be forgiven in thinking that wars might be preferable to the savage sadism of *Rollerball*. It seems to be a mixture of many contemporary sports (such as roller derby, motorcycle racing, wrestling, and pinball) but highlighting the savage aspects.

Technically the film works well on several levels from John Box's futuristic sets and André Previn's score, drawn from Tchaikovsky's *Sleeping Beauty* and Bach's *'Dorian' Toccata*—contrasting ultra-luxury and ultra-violence, respectively. However some clichés surface in the form of drugs for tranquillity and an all-knowing computer called Zero. Generally, the acting is good. I particularly liked John Houseman's Energy Executive, Bartholomew, and Sir Ralph Richardson's eccentric computer custodian. Surprisingly, Jonathan E. I found to be a little humourless and inconsistent. The tenderness he displays for a dead friend seemed at odds with the ruthless persona required to play the game. He rebelled against the system but seemed very inarticulate. However many of Caan's lines did tend to be mumbled and he may have been more articulate than I thought!

Despite these criticisms the film's cautionary notes remain valid and seem to me to be only a slightly exaggerated extrapolation of today's political and sociological problems.

[Rollerball won a BAFTA for Best Art Direction.]

Lisztomania
(Writer/Dir.: Ken Russell)

Even before the film's main release, the Liszt Society made public its objections that Liszt's music had been 're-arranged in rock style' and that the story contained scenes of rape, blood-sucking, exorcism, and castration. Indeed it does, and the music is Liszt-filtered-through-Rick Wakeman but then this is a Ken Russell film. It is one of the blackest black comedies I've ever seen and one of the most nonsensical.

Russell had a good opportunity here to create another *Music Lovers* if he'd curbed his visual excesses and modern dialogue. Instead he's gone in for another *Tommy*-style film, certainly in terms of casting. While Roger Daltrey was excellent in the latter film, he is very miscast here as Liszt. Paul Nicholas, however, makes a good Wagner and Ringo Starr is hilarious as a Scouse Pope. As in all Russell's films, the production design and photography (Peter Suschitzky) are outstanding. What this film lacks is a firm central theme and an analytical approach to the composer as he showed with *Song of Summer* for the BBC on Delius and Tchaikovsky in *The Music Lovers*. But then Melvyn Bragg wrote the screenplay for the latter; what a pity he didn't for *Lisztomania*.

[Ken Russell died in 2011.]

Legend of the Werewolf
(Dir.: Freddie Francis)

This is the latest treatment of this horror film genre. I say latest, but unfortunately this does not also mean best. However, it is a film which can be said to be redeemed by small character parts; Hugh Griffith and Renée Houston are a treat to watch as the couple who finds the young boy with lupine proclivities. David Rintoul (in his first film) has a wide-eyed air of innocence which gains our sympathy especially when we see him in the 'Belle et la Bête' climax.

Many of designer Jack Shampan's sets are reminiscent of stage and pantomime and Ron Moody's tetchy zookeeper is definitely over the top. You can see him acting every line, but his lines are not that good anyway. On the plus side, Peter Cushing gives a more than adequate performance as a pathologist. The film is said to have used a new transition process for the werewolf scenes, but apart from getting a werewolf's-eye view of things and some ultra-close-ups of sanguineous fangs, I failed to see anything unconventional technically. I would say it is a film which works in parts, but not as a whole.

The Rocky Horror Picture Show
(Dir.: Jim Sharman)

The Rocky Horror Picture Show is best described as a hybrid of *Hair*, *Flesh Gordon*, and the *Frankenstein* and *Dracula* films. It energetically attempts to send them all up both musically and visually. Based on the stage play by Richard O'Brien, the film too is rather a stagey affair, though nicely opened up to include Charles Gray as an Edgar Lustgarten-type criminologist who introduces the transvestite goings-on at a castle-like mansion.

Although the pace and songs are energetic and original, one could wish for a slightly more coherent screenplay in between them. However, the photography (Peter Suschitzky), production, and make-up design (Pierre La Roche) are of a very high standard. The film perhaps tried to do too much in too short a time and while one is never bored, one comes away feeling a tad confused, but dazzled!

Race with the Devil
(Dir.: Jack Starrett)

Race with the Devil is in many ways strongly reminiscent of *Rosemary's Baby*: satanists lurk everywhere but under oh-so-innocent guises. Although most of this film takes place outdoors, director Jack Starrett has created a very claustrophobic atmosphere by enclosing his characters in a Dormobile-type truck, which conveys them to and from the action. Peter Fonda, Loretta Switt, Warren Oates, and Lara Parker play two couples who witness a murder during a satanic ritual and spend the rest of the film trying to escape the protagonists.

The film contains some startling car chase sequences, although in a film which depends so much on tension and tempo, some do seem a little longer than they should be. The ending is not as resolved as one would hope but is nevertheless a suitable satanic one for this chilling and demonic thriller.

Bug
(Dir.: Jeannot Szwarc)

Bug concerns a plague of cockroaches which can actually set fire to objects by rubbing their hind legs together. If you're laughing already, then I would inform you that this film is not as bad as it sounds but sadly it is not as good as it could be either. After an earth tremor, the bugs emerge and cause several deaths before, mercifully, they die off naturally. Enter mad scientist Bradford Dillman who manages to breed a super bug by mating household cockroaches with the incendiary kind. Naturally, these cause more trouble than the last ones and are not disposed of so easily.

This film cries out to be compared with *Willard* or *Phase IV* (films about rats and ants going rogue, respectively) but unfortunately it is not in the same class. Despite this, the film has several funny moments, including reference to the bugs as four-legged Boy Scouts and a woman's hair catches fire as she's about to prepare '*smoked* salmon'. Ah well, you can't win them all!

1976

The Omen
(Dir.: Richard Donner)

In reviewing *The Omen*, comparisons with similar films, e.g. *The Exorcist*, are inevitable. However, *The Omen* is different in that it is the effects and not the manifestations of evil which are dealt with. Damien (Harvey Stephens) is the adopted son of Robert and Cathy Thorn (Gregory Peck and Lee Remick), an American ambassador and his wife. He seems a perfectly normal child until his fifth birthday, when a strange and terrifying sequence of events begins to happen around him. The basis of the film is a credible but controversial interpretation of the Book of Revelations ('… the beast has a human number, it is six hundred and sixty-six').

David Seltzer's screenplay is based on his novel *The Omen* and sticks fairly closely to it. Gil Taylor's muted, autumnal cinematography makes a significant contribution to the prevailing mood and Jerry Goldsmith's score evokes a chilling and sombre tone, both presaging and accompanying the terror, massaging the aural equivalent of ice onto already frazzled nerves.

[Jerry Goldsmith wrote hundreds of TV and film scores. He only won an Oscar for one, The Omen. *The Omen was remade in 2006 and released on the 6th June that year (6.6.06). In my view it was inferior to, or at best, an unnecessary addition to the original, but surprisingly, had the same screenwriter, David Seltzer. The original film featured a decapitation scene which was devised by John Richardson, a visual effects designer. On Friday, August 13th 1976, he was involved in a car accident where his passenger was beheaded. Richardson allegedly saw a road sign near the accident scene showing the distance to a Dutch town that read: Ommen, 66.6 km. Many other incidents occurred which plagued the film. Shortly before filming, Gregory Peck's son committed suicide. In the film, Peck attempts to kill his (screen) son when he realises he is the Devil incarnate; not surprisingly, he found this scene very stressful to shoot.]*

Taxi Driver
(Dir.: Martin Scorsese)

Travis Bickle (Robert De Niro), recently discharged from Vietnam, now earns his living as a cab driver in New York. Unable to sleep at night even after twelve hours' work a day, he takes on extra duty 'anytime, anywhere'. Relentlessly, his rides take him through New York's seedy nightlife; prostitutes, pimps, murderers, and rapists all come under his restless gaze. He becomes obsessed with the sordid squalor and insidiously plans a drastic purgatory operation after an encounter with a twelve-year-old prostitute played by Jodie Foster.

The music, the last score by the late Bernard Herrmann, casts a hypnotic, captivating spell over the whole film and contributes to its strange charisma. The brash neon vulgarity of the primary colours in Michael Chapman's cinematography makes it easier for us to understand Travis's repulsion for his contemporary world. Towards the end, far from hating him, we almost warm to this schizoid anti-hero. De Niro is surely heading for an Oscar nomination if not a win. The film lingers in the memory, as indeed does the thought that there are many Travis's around in today's society.

[De Niro was nominated for a Best Actor Oscar, but didn't win. Bernard Herrmann won a posthumous Oscar for his score.]

The Slipper and the Rose
(Co-writer/Dir.: Bryan Forbes)

You might think that you're too old to go and see a film about Cinderella, but why not take the plunge and see how delightful this all-British concoction is? Michael Hordern, Edith Evans, and Annette Crosbie provide comic relief, Gemma Craven and Richard Chamberlain the romantic interest, and a host of other players emotions ranging from pathos to joy. Beautifully photographed by Tony Imi, it just shows how diverse the British film industry now is as it plays alongside films like *The Man Who Fell to Earth*.

All the President's Men
(Dir.: Alan J. Pakula)

All the President's Men opens with typewriter keys exploding noisily onto white paper as they inscribe that fatal date June 17th 1972 on it. Right from the start, Alan (*Klute*) Pakula wants us to know that the type-written word is mighty powerful. This film deals with the uncovering of Watergate, told through the eyes of two *Washington Post* reporters, Bob Woodward and Carl Bernstein (Robert Redford and Dustin Hoffman), or Woodstein as they are collectively known in the film.

William Goldman's script is effective but never boring; it must have been quite a job cramming so much detail into two and a half hours of screen time yet the film never even mentions the Nixon tapes and a host of other facts which are now common knowledge. However, it does maintain suspense, suggest a sinister and insidious menace, and deals well with the understandable reluctance of the *Washington Post*'s editor to publish such devastating material. Gordon Willis's cinematography goes in for extreme contrast; the newsroom is portrayed in blazing light, no shadows or secrets anywhere, whereas the Washington streets are sleazy, menacing, dark, and suspicious. Definitely a film to see, although another is called for to deal with Nixon's reaction to Watergate.

[All the President's Men won Oscars for Best Supporting Actor (Jason Robards), Screenplay, and Best Sound. William Goldman, who also scripted Butch Cassidy and the Sundance Kid, Misery, Marathon Man, *and scores of other films, died on 16th November 2018, aged eighty-seven.]*

Silver Streak
(Dir.: Arthur Hiller)

Although it can't really make up its mind whether it's a comedy thriller or a disaster film, there are a lot of admirable things in *Silver Streak*. Gene Wilder has never been funnier, especially when jolted out of an amorous ecstasy by the abrupt manifestation of a corpse which dangles upside down at a train window, or in an aircraft piloted by a reckless farming woman swooping low over a herd of sheep that changes pattern like a rugby scrum in a state of panic. The ultimate scene, a train crash, is outstanding, with subjective views of crossing rails whizzing towards us at a fantastic speed, and the slow-motion crumbling of pillars and posts in Chicago Central Station. An undemanding piece of amicable hokum but certainly not deserving of its widespread slating by the critics. Sequels, anyone?

Network
(Dir.: Sidney Lumet)

Without question, *Network* is a writer's film. As the credits proclaim, *Network* is *by* Paddy Chayefsky (rather than the customary 'Screenplay by …' or 'Written for the screen by …'). The writer is indeed due for a new wave of acclaim and every word of the script is close to a written polished gem. The banality of television is the film's main concern though bitter asides are made about politics, religion, and in particular, large organisations and syndicates ('… these are the only nations of the world now!').

The cast includes William Holden, Faye Dunaway, and the late Peter Finch (nominated for a posthumous Oscar for his sly, amused, and self-aware performance as Howard Beale, 'the mad prophet of the tube'). His now classic line, meant to be repeated by all who heard him, shouted through an open window to the street below, 'I'm as mad as hell and I'm not going to take it any more', resonates long after the credits disappear.

The satire is sharp, the direction silky; my only criticism is that the script is at times a little too literate. Everyone, under no matter what stress, manages to meet adversity head-on with a stream of rhetoric that might make Shakespeare envious. This is indeed surprising since the characters with whom *Network* concerns itself are hardly ever supposed to read books or even a newspaper. However, this is a small carp to make in what is otherwise an extremely well-observed film.

*[*Network *won Oscars for Best Actor (Peter Finch), Best Actress (Faye Dunaway), Best Supporting Actress (Beatrice Straight), and Best Screenplay (Paddy Chayefsky). Peter Finch also received a posthumous BAFTA for Best Actor.]*

The Eagle Has Landed
(Dir.: John Sturges)

This is basically about a plot by the Germans to kill Churchill during the Second World War and is based on a Jack Higgins novel. The paring down of events and characters in Tom Mankiewicz's script has left most of them in an empty void. There is a certain tension in the ending but did the rest of the film have to sound, look, and feel as if it were bored with itself? Lethargic fare. Don't bother.

1977

Star Wars
(Writer/Dir.: George Lucas)

Imposing old-fashioned antics on newfangled gadgetry, we are led into the thick of the action by a long-written preamble like the summarised instalment of a Saturday morning matinee. All manner of tosh about interplanetary tensions and a kidnapped princess (Carrie Fisher with stereophonic false hairpieces) goes floating upwards and soon we are beset by laser rays and starships. A quaintly contrasted pair of robots, R2-D2 (Artoo-Detoo) and C-3PO (See-Threepio), provide shades of Laurel and Hardy, though the comedy wears thin after two hours and is only fitfully maintained. Luke Skywalker (Mark Hamill), damp behind the ears but of good potential, leads the human contingent, along with Han Solo (Harrison Ford), a mercenary pirate captain whose hardboiled attitudes cloak an OK heart.

The show, for me, was partly saved by Obi Wan Kenobi (Alec Guinness) and Grand Moff Tarkin (Peter Cushing), actors of the Old School, who seem to exemplify the Art of Clear Speaking. The last thirty minutes or so comprise an attack on the dreaded and colossal Death Star (pat on the back for British production designer John Barry, not the composer), a truly impressive cinematic illusion. The dog fights between the space ships are impressive but overlong, although children will no doubt disagree.

A film to see definitely, but a film to remember? Chairs drawn up to the TV for *Star Trek* or *Doctor Who* have surely rendered us blasé about such things. Or have they?

[Had 20th Century Fox turned down the script based on this review I would by now have lost them a cumulative total of about forty billion dollars! Star Wars won six Oscars: for Art Direction, Costume Design, Sound, Film Editing, Visual Effects, and Score.]

The Gauntlet
(Dir.: Clint Eastwood)

I thought I had warmed to the Eastwood genre of film by gradually introducing myself to such essays in violence as *Dirty Harry*, *The Outlaw Josey Wales*, and *Thunderbolt and Lightfoot* but I'm afraid *The Gauntlet* has switched me off again. It's exciting enough and time passes quickly, but the story, the story …

I had just managed to suspend belief at the fact that the chief of Phoenix police had ordered a key witness against him to be killed, along with her police escort, Ben Shocklee (Clint E.), when we're asked to believe that on several occasions, in an ambulance, bus, and a house, which are splattered with bullets, our gallant pair escape with but a few cuts and bruises. To top it all there is an unconvincing shoot-out with the police chief and that's when I switched off. Mr E. will no doubt be laughing all the way to his Swiss bank. Perhaps next time he can afford a better screenwriter.

The Last Remake of Beau Geste
(Writer/Dir.: Marty Feldman)

The aging Sir Hector Geste (Trevor Howard) takes a young greedy wife (Ann-Margaret) who's after his famed Blue Water sapphire but his sons Beau (Michael York) and Digby (Marty Feldman) hide the gem and join the French Foreign Legion in North Africa. This is Marty Feldman's directorial debut and the first thirty minutes or so are hilarious but thereafter, a patchy and stodgy spirit prevails, raising faint smiles rather than guffaws. Still, some nice things to savour,

Trevor Howard's randy Sir Hector who claims he's '... alive and dying', Spike Milligan plays a dotty butler, and Terry-Thomas is a not too bright prison governor. I particularly liked James Earl Jones as an Arab leader with a very upper-class English accent, don't you know.

As a rude send-up of what must be 1977's biggest flop, about the Legionnaires (*March or Die*), it could hardly be more timely and as a parody about them it is very acute, often spinning off to giddy extremes (Marty even has a scene with the late Gary Cooper). In the trailer to the film Marty says, 'Universal must be mad letting me direct and write this picture.' Not mad perhaps, just a little too optimistic?

Valentino
(Co-writer/Dir.: Ken Russell)

Ken Russell has always treated facts with a very elastic dramatic licence. His treatment of Rudolf Valentino's life is no exception. His approach to *Valentino* when the star is thrown in prison, among thieves, pimps, and drunks, and a malicious jailer deprives him of toilet privileges, with degrading consequences, seems unlikely. One cannot believe it really happened like that, but who can deny it might have *felt* that bad to Valentino?

The screenplay is arranged in flashback from the 'lying in state' that followed Valentino's death in 1926. The pace slackens a little but a high style is often maintained from Philip Harrison's sumptuous sets to Shirley Russell's (Ken's wife) evocative costumes. However, the film's quality is hinged to the interpretation of Valentino, given in his first acting-with-words assignment by Rudolf Nureyev. Despite what the critics said I didn't think his acting was all that bad, although I'm sure he prefers his ballet dancing. Felicity Kendal gives a good performance as June Mathis, the screenwriter instrumental in Valentino's movie success.

Valentino's life and career, I think was sadly ironic. On screen, he was a passionate and forceful lover, but off it, a drifting, insecure shell. His death scene, a solo set piece, has the feel of a ballet, attempting to grasp an orange from the floor, perhaps symbolic of the good and natural life (a failed dream to own an orange grove) that he had in

14

mind before stardom. Although I was pleasantly surprised by this film, I don't believe it is Russell's best. For me that was *The Music Lovers.*

Close Encounters of the Third Kind
(Dir.: Steven Spielberg)

At the time of writing *Close Encounters of the Third Kind* (*CE3K*) and *Star Wars* are being shown in neighbouring cinemas. *Star Wars* looks a bit like a strip cartoon in comparison to *CE3K*. While the former is set all over the galaxy, the latter is firmly earthbound, apart from the last twenty minutes or so when a UFO and its alien contents are revealed for all to see. It is this sequence that has made the film so popular, with over eighteen months spent on designing, let alone creating the special effects required for a large extra-terrestrial ship to materialise out of the clouds and dock on a lonely mountainside. A truly impressive sight thanks to Doug Trumbull and his effects team. The film boasts six directors of photography, one each for the mothership, the UFOs, American, Indian, and studio sequences, and extra-terrestrials.

With so much heavy emphasis on the visuals, one could expect the human element to be rather depleted. Not the case, as Richard Dreyfuss and Francois Truffaut give convincing and credible performances as Roy Nealy, the electrical engineer who meets the aliens, and Lacombe the French scientist, who attempts to decode their signals comprising colour and music. Note that throughout the film Lacombe has to be subtitled and interpreted in contrast to the splendidly direct communication between alien and scientist at the end. Steven (*Jaws*) Spielberg's done it again!

[CE3K won an Oscar for Best Cinematography and a BAFTA for Production Design.]

Communion
(Co-writer/Dir.: Alfred Sole)

Communion is unashamedly Hitchcockian in style and technique from the *Psycho*-esque knife attacks to the protracted death sequence à la

15

Torn Curtain—and the actors are refreshingly dispensable throughout. All the cast look guilty or dead in the best traditions of the maestro. The story, co-written by Sole and Rosemary Ritvo, is set in 1961 in Paterson, New Jersey and concerns a problem child, Alice, whose pranks arouse suspicion that she has murdered her sister Karen. There seems little doubt of her guilt, particularly when her mean Aunt Annie is stabbed in the feet when walking downstairs (a very gory scene; smelling salts are recommended). However, all is not as it seems and eventually the real villain is unmasked. We are still left with the tension of whether there will be a neat, happy ending (I won't tell you). To confuse matters further, there is an obscenely obese lodger, a devout housekeeper, and a befuddled priest. The score (by Stephen Lawrence) is worthy of anything that Bernard Herrmann produced for Hitchcock and the whole film is as crisp and taut and neat as anything the maestro did.

*[*Communion *was renamed* Alice, Sweet Alice *after its release.]*

Looking for Mr. Goodbar
(Writer/Dir.: Richard Brooks)

Diane Keaton recently won a BAFTA for best actress in Woody Allen's film, *Annie Hall*. She deserves one too as Theresa Dunn in *Looking for Mr. Goodbar*. Based on Judith Rossner's bestselling novel, it concerns the daughter of a malcontent Catholic family. Her sister is sluttish and marries outside her faith but Theresa teaches deaf children by day yet spends her nights cruising the singles bars, picking up men and taking them back to her sordid flat. Her affairs become wilder, more psychotic, and eventually she starts to take cocaine. Socially laudable by day and reprehensible at night, her schizophrenic character is reflected by 'mirrors'—her family, her background, her lovers. Brooks uses flashbacks and flash-forwards a mite too often and they are rather too self-explanatory but the fluid nature of the editing (George Glenville) is exemplary.

For a fairly liberated woman, it is puzzling that she has no women friends to confide in. The climax is predictable but horrifying in both the novel and film and I should warn viewers about heavy use of stroboscopic-style editing towards the end. I was a little disappointed at the abrupt ending, but it seems that violence, inexorable as it was in this reckless venture, is not so much Theresa's retribution, but a warning that needs to be heeded before people look for their Mr or Ms Goodbar.

The Spy Who Loved Me
(Dir.: Lewis Gilbert)

Can a lighter than air script compete with grandiose art direction? The makers of this latest Bond film seem to think so but their efforts don't quite succeed. The plot, as usual, concerns a villain (Stromberg played by Curt Jurgens), hell-bent on destroying the world and building a new underwater one. The plot is derivative, a sort of *You Only Live Twice* with submarines instead of rockets, with a nice nubile spy (Barbara Bach), an underwater car, and a sort of giant hyper bathysphere. Stromberg is dispatched far too early in the proceedings in very un-Bond-like fashion (plain old shooting); better luck is Richard Kiel, a seven-foot villain with bionic teeth, a remarkably indestructible foe for Bond (Roger Moore).

Nothing in the film quite lives up to the spectacular ski jump in the prologue or the visually ravishing titles with silhouetted girls clambering over a gun. Bond films tend to be critic-proof and it is enjoyable, but leave your critical faculties at home. The real star of the Bond films has always been, and probably will always be, the production designer, Ken Adam.

Film reviews in *Tabloid*, the newspaper of The Wellcome Foundation Ltd.

I worked for The Wellcome Foundation from 1978–1995 but only started to write for *Tabloid* in 1988. This was the first time I wrote about travel and was pleased and surprised by the comments I received from people within the company (whom I hadn't met before) who had travelled to the same places.

1988

A Cry in the Dark
(Dir.: Fred Schepisi)

If the idea of a modern-day witch-hunt in 1980s Australia seems an unlikely one to you, then *A Cry in the Dark* will convince you otherwise. This is the true story of Lindy Chamberlain who, whilst on holiday near Ayers Rock, saw a dingo leave their family tent and later found her nine-week-old baby, Azaria, missing.

Lindy was accused of murder and jailed and the film grippingly reconstructs the blows dealt to the Chamberlains by dubious forensic evidence, intense media distortion, and the public's insatiable demand for scapegoats.

Lindy is played by the impeccable Meryl Streep and it isn't just her Australian accent that impresses, it is her whole persona as the luckless, apparently hard-faced Lindy. Sam Neill as her husband, Michael, is also superb and slowly develops from a trusting, deeply religious man (a minister for the Seventh Day Adventists) to a more suspicious and timid character.

It is difficult to describe this as a film to enjoy, but I regard it as an important one in alerting us to the pervasive and distorting influences of the media in our lives.

There is also one very important character missing in the credits: Australia itself. Ayers Rock, where it all happened, is spectacularly captured in Ian Baker's photography, all peering, probing aerial shots and telescoped zooms, whilst Bruce Smeaton's score is hauntingly apt. If Streep, Neill, et al. aren't Oscar nominated for this one, I'll eat my Film 88 T-shirt. (Well, I would if I had one!)

Gorillas in the Mist
(Dir.: Michael Apted)

In December 1966, Dian Fossey left the comfort and privilege of America to live in the mountains of Central Africa to observe and preserve wild mountain gorillas. Her story is told in *Gorillas in the Mist*. Aided mainly by a devoted native tracker, Dian (superbly played by Sigourney Weaver) shuns both material and, eventually, emotional comforts, despite a promising relationship with *National Geographic* photographer Bob Campbell (Bryan Brown).

Her interactions with the gorillas are, by turn, scary and endearing. Although the credits reveal the presence of 'mime artists', Rick Baker's astonishingly realistic simian make-up designs ensure that you won't spot the difference between actors and gorillas.

Although a shade leisurely at times, the beauty of Africa, Fossey's single-minded devotion, and the superb creatures remain long in the memory after the final credits. Dian Fossey was brutally murdered in 1985; the identity of her murderer or murderers remains a mystery to this day.

Apartment Zero
(Writer/Dir.: Martin Donovan)

This film was given very little publicity and only a short run on its general release; a pity since it is an unusual thriller, claustrophobically combining psychological and political themes which continually keep one on tenterhooks. It stars Colin Firth as Adrian LeDuc, a shy, neurotic and reclusive bachelor who tries to eke out a living by screening films at a cinema he has rented. His small apartment becomes more and more like a prison and to help pay his exorbitant rent, he decides to take a lodger. Enter Jack Carney (Hart Bochner), a charismatic American, but Adrian discovers he is not the saviour (and possibly potential lover) he thought he would be.

The tension developing between Adrian and Jack is played out against a background of political killings (the film is set in Buenos Aires). Neighbours Dora Bryan and Liz Smith provide a little light relief as eccentric sisters after they've been at the sherry bottle a little too long. The film could have ended at about four different points and it will certainly keep you on the edge of your seat to the very end. Patricia Highsmith would have loved it; there are shades of Tom Ripley in Adrian's character but the film stands alone as a minor classic.

Willow
(Dir.: Ron Howard)

Fantasy, adventure, and myth are blended into a very acceptable recipe in Ron Howard's *Willow*. Willow is a member of the peaceful, diminutive Nelwyn race who find a special baby, Elora Danan, who is destined to cause the downfall of wicked Queen Bavmorda (Jean Marsh). The fates call upon Willow (Warwick Davis) and an unlikely outcast warrior, Madmartigan (Val Kilmer), to battle against evil adversaries in order to carry Elora Danan to the safety of castle Tir Asleen.

Adrian Biddle's rich-toned cinematography makes the most of the spectacular New Zealand landscapes and North Wales and with eighty stuntmen featured in the credits, one is hardly short-changed as far as the action goes, in particular a stunningly photographed toboggan ride over huge crevasses. There is always something to please the retina even if, at 125 minutes, the film is a shade too long. There is a nice love-hate relationship between Val Kilmer and Joanne Whalley who plays Queen Bavmorda's daughter and the splendid Patricia Hayes is also good value as the sorceress Raziel. It never ceases to amaze me how Ron Howard (boy-next-door Ricky Cunningham in TV's *Happy Days*) has managed to graduate so quickly to direct films such as *Splash*, *Cocoon*, and now, *Willow*. I'm sure it won't be long before he's directing another major movie.

Young Guns
(Dir.: Chris Cain)

There seems to be a consensus view that after *Butch Cassidy and the Sundance Kid,* the cinema Western died. Recent attempts to revive it, like the depressing *Silverado* for example, have not had the required Lazarus-like effect. *Young Guns* may well have the required credentials to do so, as it interweaves the Brat Pack actors with the legend of Billy the Kid. Immigrant Englishman John Tunstall (Terence Stamp) struggles to establish himself as a successful rancher and enlists the aid of six youngsters (Kiefer Sutherland, Charlie Sheen, Emilio Estevez, Lou Diamond Phillips, Dermot Mulroney, and Casey Siemaszko) as 'Regulators' to help him.

Tunstall's rival, L. G. Murphy (Jack Palance in truly evil mode), has pocketed the local sheriff to ensure that he remains the sole cattle baron in Lincoln County. A cowardly ambush results in Tunstall's murder and the gang of six declare war on Murphy and his gang. Only later do they realise that their latest member is William Bonney alias Billy the Kid (an excellent portrayal of psychopathic glee by Estevez). Gritty and grainy, filtered-through-Worcester-sauce cinematography contributes greatly to the prevailing mood, as do the action sequences. Whether you like Westerns, the Brat Pack, both or neither, I think you will welcome this attempt to resurrect the genre.

Who Framed Roger Rabbit
(Dir.: Robert Zemeckis)

In *Who Framed Roger Rabbit,* private eye Eddie Valiant (Bob Hoskins) finds himself involved in a murder case in which the chief suspect is Roger Rabbit, a star of cartoon films.

Eddie is helped on his frenetic and bizarre quest by Jessica, Roger's sexy wife, but they have strong opposition from the heinous Judge Doom (Christopher Lloyd). He has a penchant for dipping the 'toons' cartoon characters in a mixture of turps, acetone, and benzene, the only thing that will eliminate them!

The technical wizardry of the whole enterprise is very impressive thanks to Director of Animation Richard Williams and his vast team. (Incidentally he designed Wellcome's Calpol TV adverts too, together with two of the title sequences of the *Pink Panther* films.) However, the plot line is rather weak, the overall tenor too loud and frenetic, Roger Rabbit's voice too shrill and irritating, and the 104 minutes seem more like 200.

There are two redeeming treats: the pre-credit sequence which just involves the 'toons' and distils the very best of *Tom and Jerry*-like capers. Secondly, the nightclub sequence where Jessica (voiced by Kathleen Turner) polishes Stubby Kaye's head whilst Bob Hoskins' eyes are out like organ stops is a coup de cinema. Those who stay to watch the end credits will spot people listed as 'effects inbetweeners', whatever they are! Answers on a postcard to Barry Norman, not me, please …

[*This review was written for* Tabloid, *the newspaper of The Wellcome Foundation Ltd, makers of Calpol at that time. Hence my reference to its TV ads here. Sadly Bob Hoskins died in 2014.* Who Framed Roger Rabbit *won Oscars for Film Editing, Sound Effects Editing, and Visual Effects, and won a BAFTA for Visual Effects.*]

1989

Shirley Valentine
(Dir.: Lewis Gilbert)

A sort of extension to his *Educating Rita,* Willy Russell now gives us *Shirley Valentine,* an equally riveting blend of comedy and pathos. Pauline Collins (reprising her stage role) is superb as Shirley, the housewife who has Gotten Into a Rut and Wants To Discover Herself.

Sentenced to urban drudgery at the kitchen sink with a semi-mute, clock-watching spouse (Bernard Hill), who goes berserk if he doesn't get his meals on time, Shirley escapes to the Greek island of Mykonos with her friend (Alison Steadman). She finds liberation with Costas (Tom Conti), a tavern keeper, but then realises that she hasn't fallen in love with him, but with Living. It is a film that so easily could have veered into sentimentality but never does, thanks to Russell's acerbic wit and Collins' portrayal, often with pieces to camera as if speaking directly to you. We can all learn something from *Shirley Valentine*; don't miss it.

Batman
(Dir.: Tim Burton)

Unless you've spent the last few months on a desert island you've probably not escaped the hype and fanfares for *Batman,* the largest grossing film to date. Is it worth it? Yes and no. Yes, because of the delightful, zany, deliciously evil performance of Jack Nicholson as Batman's adversary, the Joker. Yes, because of Anton Furst's dark and chokingly claustrophobic set designs for Gotham City, an urban nightmare of a place that would probably give Prince Charles apoplexy.

And the no's? Well, Michael Keaton is a perfectly adequate Batman and Bruce Wayne. The only problem is, he doesn't seem to get an awful lot to do in the film. Jack Nicholson has all the best lines and seems to dominate every scene—even the ones where he doesn't actually appear in the frame. To be generous, as a basic tale of Good versus Evil, it will surely do and as the cash registers keep ringing, *Batman 2* is already in production.

[Anton Furst received an Oscar for Best Art Direction for Batman. *Sadly, Furst committed suicide in 1991. He designed only one other film after* Batman, Awakenings, *starring Robin Williams as neurologist Oliver Sacks.]*

Wilt
(Dir.: Michael Tuchner)

Based on Tom Sharpe's bestseller, *Wilt* has, like its source material, its fair share of belly laughs and farcical misunderstandings. Aiding and abetting this hilarious farrago is Griff Rhys Jones as Wilt, the downtrodden polytechnic lecturer, Mel Smith as the luckless Inspector

Flint, and Alison Steadman as the martial arts-obsessed health freak, Eva Wilt.

I won't give away too much of the plot, save to say it involves an inflatable doll, a serial strangler, and more misunderstandings than a Whitehall farce. Take no notice of those critics who gave *Wilt* a critical pasting; go and exercise your chuckle muscles forthwith!

When Harry Met Sally
(Dir.: Rob Reiner)

Can men and women really stay friends without sex getting in the way? This is the theme of *When Harry Met Sally*. To say that it is an engaging comedy doesn't really do it justice since it is far more than this. Intercut with scenes of elderly couples explaining how they got hitched (it was never love at first sight), the film has a semi-documentary air about it.

The Harry of the title is played by Billy Crystal (of *Soap*) and Sally by the superb Meg Ryan. They first met at university where they studied journalism and their on-off relationship over the next decade or so is what the film tracks so pithily. This reviewer has now ditched Meryl Streep as his favourite actress and replaced her with Meg Ryan. One odd observation from the end credits: Mr Crystal and Ms Ryan were allocated two make-up artists each—surely their good looks need the minimum of artificial embellishment?

[After seeing the monosyllabic and frankly rude Ms Ryan on a chat show with Parkinson a few years ago, Ms Streep has now been reinstated to her former pedestal by this reviewer!]

Parenthood
(Dir.: Ron Howard)

Parenthood is a bittersweet comedy confection from the director of *Splash* and *Willow*. It attempts to deal with the problems and joys of parenthood and does so with an amusing (if sometimes patchy) blend of slapstick and reality. Gil (Steve Martin) has a son undergoing psychiatric treatment, his sister (Dianne Wiest) has a daughter who elopes with a hot-rod driver (Keanu Reeves); Gil's brother Larry (Tom Hulce) is a constant gambler and has fathered a black child, whilst his brother-in-law (Rick Moranis) teaches Kafka to this three-year-old daughter.

Choicest of all though is Gran (Helen Shaw) whose poignant analogy of life as a rollercoaster is also visually expressed in a queasily photographed scene of a chaotic children's stage play. One wonders where the joys of parenthood could possibly be in that lot but they are there, believe it or not. There are a few overlong fantasy sequences and slightly uneven tilting of the comedy/pathos axis which American TV sitcoms tend to do so well. Worth seeing.

Black Rain
(Dir.: Ridley Scott)

Black Rain sees Michael Douglas (as New York cop Nick Conklin) trailing a vicious criminal through the streets of Osaka. As a hard-bitten cop, Douglas is credible, although it's Charlie (Andy Garcia) who impresses as his ebullient sidekick. Unfortunately, Charlie the cop gets the chop rather too early in the proceedings and this activates a trail of revenge-mode action which is almost *Rambo*-esque in its intensity. Underneath the glossy veneer (Jan de Bont's camera seems to daub neon, smoke, and streaming shafts of light everywhere), this is a rather routine thriller with 2D characters. It's never boring but the individual set pieces don't seem to make a satisfying whole.

The film has done very well in Japan which is surprising when one considers the amount of abuse Douglas churns out against his Japanese counterparts.

Licence to Kill
(Dir.: John Glen)

Recently released on video, *Licence to Kill* is the sixteenth Bond film and the second to feature Timothy Dalton as Bond. It is also the first film not to use a Fleming title but tends to rehash bits of the earlier novels. Essentially the plot concerns Bond's efforts to track down an evil drug baron, Sanchez (a splendidly craggy study of psychopathy by Robert Davi). All the usual ingredients are present—a gripping pre-credit sequence, snazzy titles, superb stunts, exotic locations, and attractive girls (Talisa Soto, Carey Lowell). However I think the film is a good half hour too long and a little more humour would have certainly helped the proceedings. The film carries a 15 certificate (previous ones were PG) and the stylised menace of the earlier Bonds are now replaced by far nastier dispatches.

As an ardent Bond fan, I can only award 006 for this 007 and I hope the next one will fully restore his licence to thrill.

War of the Roses
(Dir.: Danny DeVito)

Although the title *War of the Roses* tends to conjure up a somewhat medieval or military sounding theme, the film is actually about a disintegrating marriage, although in this case, the military reference is quite apt. Oliver and Barbara Rose (Michael Douglas and Kathleen Turner) are blissfully married until one day Barbara suddenly realises that she would be much happier if Oliver was dead.

From that point onwards the bliss descends into chaos and the set pieces, including a disastrous dinner party and car battles on the lawn, climax with a taut, nerve-wracking finale on a chandelier.

Danny DeVito narrates and directs in his latest venture and in addition plays the part of Oliver's divorce lawyer, a role that he acts out with some relish. I shall watch the marriage and divorce statistics with interest over the next few months, for what *Marathon Man* did for dental appointments, *The War of the Roses* will probably do for marriage!

Uncle Buck
(Writer/Dir.: John Hughes)

Looking at times like a male caricature of Margaret Rutherford, John Candy inhabits the endearing mantle of fun-loving bachelor Uncle Buck. When Buck is left in charge of his young nephews and nieces, he starts microwaving the laundry when the washing machine won't work, feeds the dog five times a day, and prepares gargantuan breakfasts from yesterday's leftovers. Zany humour certainly abounds, but the hub of the film is the battle of wills that takes place between Buck and his teenage niece, Tia (played as a very nasty piece of work by Jean Kelly).

Both are very strong personalities and after several clashes (some of them rather nasty for a comedy), they both begin to mature somewhat towards the end of the film. The other siblings, Miles and Maizy (Macaulay Culkin and Gaby Hoffman), are a constant boon and provide several guffaws, notably a quick first line of consecutive questioning between Buck and Miles.

Uncle Buck has done well at the US box office and a thirteen-part TV series is now planned. I hope that this does not dilute the humour of the film too much.

Crimes and Misdemeanours
(Writer/Dir.: Woody Allen)

Woody Allen's latest film *Crimes and Misdemeanours* is really two films in one. A successful New York ophthalmologist (Martin Landau) decides to have his mistress (Anjelica Huston) killed because she intends to tell his wife (Claire Bloom) about their affair. Meanwhile, in another part of the city, Cliff Stern (Woody Allen) has marriage problems of his own and starts an affair with a film producer (Mia Farrow). Allen's brother in the film (Alan Alda) plays a loathsome Hollywood type who gives Woody the opportunity to make a documentary about him.

These two strands of plot do come together briefly at the end but one puzzles throughout how the merge is about to be achieved and why. The film is well written and acted but I find it difficult to decide whether I liked it. Admired might be a better word; see what you think.

Sea of Love
(Dir.: Harold Becker)

This is a taut thriller with Frank Keller (Al Pacino) playing a cop dealing with a mid-life crisis, the bottle, and loneliness. When investigating a murder, he has three vital clues, a lipstick-smeared cigarette, a wanted advert the dead man placed in a newspaper, and a perfect set of fingerprints. Immediate suspicion falls on a vengeful woman (Ellen Barkin) who answered his lonely hearts personal advertisement. He falls in love with the prime murder suspect (Barkin), believing at any time he could be the next victim. The tension present during the last twenty minutes is almost unbearable.

Honey, I Shrunk the Kids
(Dir.: Joe Johnston)

Parents may often wish they could shrink their children when they get out of hand but I wonder if they realise the problems they'd face if they actually could! You can find out in Disney's latest offering *Honey, I Shrunk the Kids*. An eccentric inventor (Rick Moranis) devises a ray which can shrink objects and one day it accidentally converts his offspring and those of his neighbours to Tom Thumb size.

The bulk of the film deals with their attempts to cross the garden (a veritable jungle) to return to the house after they were ejected with the rubbish. The seamless special effects are superb and include an eyebrow-raising flight on the back of a bee, a ride on top of a friendly ant, and a truly scary encounter with a scorpion. The set designs are beautiful as well as convincing and the whole film is a nice antidote to a recent stream of violent Stallone/Eastwood films, yet still manages to be exciting.

1990

The Hunt for Red October
(Dir.: John McTiernan)

At 136 minutes, there are times when *The Hunt for Red October* feels as if November, December, and January have been added in too. It's too long by at least two minutes but for the most part, this Cold War thriller rattles along nicely. Sean Connery stars as Captain Marko Ramius, the Soviet captain of a new submarine (Red October) that is virtually undetectable to sonar. Ramius and a small crew of like-minded fellow officers decide to defect to the West. The Americans, perhaps somewhat understandably, begin to fear the worst as the submarine speeds its way towards the US coastline. The Russians, meanwhile, are determined that their submarine is not going to fall into American hands. The plot is apparently based on a true incident but for the sake of accuracy I shall also say it's based on a Tom Clancy novel.

Sean Connery, complete with Scots accent and a can't-see-the-join toupee, is credible as Ramius and has good support from Sam Neill as Borodin, his second-in-command, and Alec Baldwin as the CIA agent. Special effects buffs may wish to know that the underwater sequences were filmed without water and used smoke to simulate fluid flow.

*[*The Hunt for Red October *won an Oscar for Sound Effects Editing.]*

Total Recall
(Dir.: Paul Verhoeven)

Take a short story by Philip K. Dick (*We Can Remember It for You Wholesale*), set three screenwriters to inflate it to nearly two hours of screen time, add eight million dollars for the budget, Arnold Schwarzenegger as Mars construction worker Doug Quaid, and you have *Total Recall*. Quaid is haunted by recurring dreams of life on Mars and decides the mystery must lie on the red planet, and gets involved in a bitter and violent struggle between the mining

29

corporation overseers and the radiation-mutated miners who seek to liberate themselves from their influence.

Not since *Dune* has so much been spent on a sci-fi film and although *Total Recall* is paced at supersonic speed, I think *Dune*, for me, was a superior film.

Dick Tracy
(Dir.: Warren Beatty)

As with *Batman,* the hype for *Dick Tracy* has been inescapable. Again, I'm afraid, we have something here that is very high in style and weak in content. Beatty, in his custard-coloured fedora and coat, may look like the cartoon character that Chester Gould created in the thirties but a little more expression behind those eyes would not come amiss. Madonna, on the other hand, as nightclub singer Breathless Mahoney, acquits herself well and her rendition of Sondheim's songs is excellent.

As in *Batman,* it is the forces of evil that capture the attention. Here they are headed by Al Pacino as Big Man; an assortment of stars such as Dustin Hoffmann and James Caan are his co-henchmen. Most are covered in layers of latex make-up so thick that recognition becomes impossible. The plot, such as it is, is rather a weary, long drawn out gangsterland battle with an unconvincing denouement. Compensations come from the rich primary colours in Vittorio Storaro's cinematography and Richard Sylbert's fantastic set designs. Had as much care been lavished on the script, then *Dick Tracy* would be a worthy success, and not what it is at the moment, a success based on hype.

[Dick Tracy won Oscars for Make-up, Music, and Original Song and won BAFTAs for Make-up and Production Design.]

The Krays
(Dir.: Peter Medak)

Surfacing after a delay of four years, *The Krays* was well worth the wait. It stars Gary and Martin Kemp (of Spandau Ballet) as the psychopathic (and often telepathic) twins, Ronnie and Reggie Kray, gangland leaders of the East End in the 50s and 60s. Screenwriter (and children's author) Philip Ridley has essayed the hypothesis that it was their fostering in an intensely matriarchal family, headed by their domineering mother Vi (a sizzling performance by Billie Whitelaw) that may have triggered their psychopathy. This simplistic and unorthodox equating of 'mother-love' leading to 'people-hate' is somewhat confusing. One could not even equate it with Ronnie's homosexuality since only he, and not his brother, was thus inclined. Also, their other brother, Charles (the film's technical adviser) is not portrayed as having any criminal or other proclivities, although he did serve a prison sentence as an accessory to the crimes his brothers committed.

The Krays is a violent, one-sided (no police are shown), and often episodic film, but despite this, the performances throughout are excellent. The whole film has a gnawing tension, subtly underlined by Michael Kamen's score, which chills the blood as effectively as any encounter with the Krays.

Nuns on the Run
(Dir.: Jonathan Lynn)

Not since *Clockwise* has there been a British comedy one can enthusiastically recommend. Whilst not quite up to its standard, *Nuns on the Run* provides some welcome laughs. Eric Idle and Robbie Coltrane play two bank robbers who steal money from the Triads and hide away in a nunnery. Disguised as nuns, they have to integrate themselves into the life of the convent and most of the film's laughs arise from there. Eric Idle has to take a religious affairs class (whilst knowing nothing about religion) whilst Robbie Coltrane takes a basketball class with great relish, not to mention some torturous moments in the shower room afterwards.

There is an energetic soundtrack from Yello and if you switch your critical faculties to medium low, you'll enjoy it!

Film Reviews from *Respect* magazine, the in-house magazine of Zeneca (1997–1998)

I worked at Zeneca from 1995–2000; it later became AstraZeneca and I worked for them until 2005. I believe *Respect* was not published after 1998 after it merged with Astra to form AstraZeneca.

1997

Titanic
(Writer/Dir.: James Cameron)

If *Titanic* had been a flop, how the critics would have loved to bring out their puns: 'sinks without trace', 'epic fails to float', etc. would have graced the tabloid headlines. However, *Titanic*, the most expensive film ever made, has already recouped its $200 million budget. Most of this will undoubtedly have gone on the excellent visual effects (by Digital Domain), the production design (by Peter Lamont, long a stalwart of Bond movie sets), and no doubt, a great deal of waterproof make-up for the cast. Binding elements of the film together is (initially anyway) a somewhat crass love story that makes Barbara Cartland's output look classy. Jack Dawson (Leonardo DiCaprio), an itinerant artist travelling steerage, meets Rose Bukater (Kate Winslet), a well-to-do American girl from first class. This relationship encapsulates the differences between the classes on board the ship, in particular the exchanges between Rose's fiancé (Billy Zane) and Jack. This focus on two (fictional) people was probably Cameron's way of creating an emotional bond between the audience and the film. After all, everyone knows how it will end, but they don't know which of the two (if any) will survive.

The emotions one feels towards these two were no doubt meant to spill over for the 1,500 souls which perished. The last scenes between Winslet and DiCaprio are the most moving in the film and will probably send shares in the Kleenex Corporation rocketing. The mere word Titanic has now become a metaphor for any sort of disaster that befalls mankind. This film may be a disaster movie but is by no means a movie disaster.

*[*Titanic *won eleven Oscars: for Best Picture, Direction, Cinematography, Costume Design, Art Direction, Sound, Editing, Visual Effects, Score, Original Song, and Best Actress (Kate Winslet).]*

1998

The Truman Show
(Dir.: Peter Weir)

I tend to be wary of any film starring Jim Carrey, his maniacal glee often failing to hit my humour receptors. Not so in *The Truman Show*, where his mania is toned down and is substituted with a pensive and disturbing paranoia. With good cause, for his character, Truman Burbank, realises that not everything is as it seems in the idyllic town of Seahaven where he lives. After a series of small but revealing incidents he realises that his every move is being filmed and indeed has been filmed since he was born. He is the star of a worldwide TV hit called *The Truman Show* and every single character in his life is an extra or an actor, including his wife (Laura Linney).

There are some serious flaws which occur to one afterwards, e.g. why has he not seen himself on TV or even read about his fame in a newspaper? More illogical perhaps is the relief which the TV audience expresses when Truman finds out the truth. Do they really want his hit TV show to end? Nevertheless, Peter (*Picnic at Hanging Rock, Mosquito Coast*) Weir's film is so compellingly watchable that these thoughts only occur to one later on. Worth watching, even if you're not a Carrey fan.

*[*The Truman Show *won BAFTAs for Best Screenplay, Production Design, and Direction.]*

Saving Private Ryan
(Dir.: Steven Spielberg)

The opening sequence of *Saving Private Ryan*, the D-day landing at Omaha, lasts some twenty-five minutes and in this time brings the audience closer to a vision of hell than one would have thought possible. The brutal carnage and deafening noises assault the senses and one is paralysed with awe at the massive loss of life. The core of the film is based on a quest to find Private Ryan (Matt Damon), the sole survivor of three brothers killed in action during the war. Tom Hanks plays John Miller, the captain of the small troupe of soldiers detailed to find him, and gives one of the most authoritative performances of his career.

The film will no doubt garner a handful of Oscars. One should certainly go to Janusz Kamiński's desaturated photography, colour deliberately haemorrhaged from each frame as if presaging and echoing the fate of so many soldiers who died.

[Saving Private Ryan won five Oscars: Direction, Cinematography, Sound, Editing, and Sound Effects, and won BAFTAs for Sound and Special Effects.]

Letters and Review Published in Film and Video Magazines

I have always been an inveterate letter writer and film and video magazines were often the recipients of my outpourings. I believe it was the *ABC Film Review* (later called *Film Review*) that received most of my output and a published letter or a correctly completed crossword was rewarded with several free tickets to the ABC or Odeon cinemas. Below are a selection of published letters and a review.

Losing the Plot

Whilst *The Bourne Ultimatum* is a high octane thriller which does credit to the modern art of film editing, I found the plot to have more holes than a piece of Gruyère cheese. Are we seriously to believe that the CIA building would allow Jason Bourne to enter it without anyone recognising or detaining him? Would thhave not changed the code on his pass, and how did he enter Noah Vosen's office unnoticed? To keep something like the Blackbriar document in an office safe seemed unlikely, and it would have been more credible for Bourne to have hacked into a computer file from a remote location. Not one, but three screenwriters were involved in the script. Surely one of them could have raised and addressed these points?

[Published in Film Review, *October 2007.]*

The Mirror Crack'd (Review)

After the opulence of such Brabourne/Goodwin productions like *Murder on the Orient Express* and *Death on the Nile*, it is strange to see what is, in effect, a low-key production such as *The Mirror Crack'd*. No boats, trains, or exotic locations here, merely a small country village in 1950s England. The money for this production though, went not on the sets or locale, but the stars: Elizabeth Taylor, Rock Hudson, Tony Curtis, Kim Novak, Geraldine Chaplin, Edward

Fox, and Angela Lansbury ... fees for La Taylor alone I'm sure amounting to the total cost for *Nile* or *Orient*?

As always, a murder occurs in an enclosed community and red herrings are scattered with the usual aplomb. Amidst the slightly stodgy and not particularly imaginative plot, redeeming treats include: a cheery inspector who's also a keen film buff (Edward Fox), a hale and hearty Miss Marple (Angela Lansbury), bitchy, vitriolic dialogue between Novak and Taylor ('... what a lovely figure ... and you've added so much to it.'), and Christopher Challis's scintillating photography, almost good enough to smell the countryside with.

I won't reveal the plot twists and turns, always a risky area with Christie stories. Although I basically enjoyed *The Mirror Crack'd*, I couldn't help wondering why it was, after Edward Fox spent half the film looking for clues, his aunt, Miss Marple, solves the mystery after hardly leaving her cottage!

[Published in Video Review, *April 1982. I won the princely sum of £10 for its publication; today the amount would be worth about £34. I didn't let it change my life however!]*

Syrup and Lemon

After hearing Gavin Millar extolling the virtues of Scorsese's *New York, New York* on BBC's *Arena Cinema* and mentioning the director's dismay with the bad reviews he received in the UK, I decided to see for myself whether a mass underrating had occurred. As a firm admirer of *Taxi Driver*, *Mean Streets*, and *Alice Doesn't Live Here Any More*, I must confess that the syrup and lemon juice sentiments of *New York, New York* are blended uneasily and indigestibly together in this latest effort. De Niro and Minnelli try so very hard (too hard?) to make the thing gel but I felt no empathy at all with the outcome of their clashes. The perverse up-in-the-air ending doesn't help much either. Perhaps I couldn't penetrate the thick veneer of gloss: László Kovács' camerawork—all burnished reds and browns—and Boris Leven's voluptuous set designs were so elegant. The only trouble was the actors kept getting in front of them!

New York, New York should press nostalgic buttons for Garland fans, or anyone over the age of thirty-five, but, for me, it only elicited a mild boredom. I did wake up for the main number though, which I kept humming all the way home from the cinema!

[Published in Films and Filming, *1977.]*

Riding High

Having seen *Sky Riders* recently, I must confess to a certain amazement at the film's lukewarm reception by the critics. It may not be a masterpiece of screenwriting, but the aerial sequences were more than adequate compensation (and the credits boasted three cinematographers).

I cheered (silently) at the sheer excitement of it all, and can't recall ever having sweatier palms and vertigo whilst sitting in a cinema seat. At least it shows the versatility of director Douglas Hickox, who also gave us *Entertaining Mr Sloane*.

[Published in Film Review, *1976.]*

Carry On Ice Hockey?

I approached *Slap Shot* with some trepidation, having read some critics' reports that the language was obscene and the action bordering on the violent. Well, yes—there are a lot of four-letter words, but in the sporty, dressing-room atmosphere which pervades the film, this seems to be quite natural, and ultimately inoffensive. I find it intriguing that *Slap Shot* was scripted by a woman (Nancy Dowd)— perhaps she wished to show that women can write as toughly as men, more toughly judging by some of the script.

The action too, is not for the squeamish, but neither is men's ice hockey in real life and the frenetic aspects of the sport are nimbly shot (about a millimetre above the ice) and well edited (Dede Allen heading for an Oscar shouldn't wonder); laughs and gasps intermingle constantly. The striptease finale was riotously funny, especially the quick glances at the crowd's reactions, notably a little old lady with her binoculars to hand. Paul Newman and Strother Martin were in fine form as the coach and manager of the Chiefs, respectively. A subplot involving Newman's divorce was less successful. On the whole, a very funny film which I can only describe as a sort of *Carry On Ice Hockey.*

[Published in Film Review, *1977.]*

No Flesh in the Pan

One critic recently stated how feeble *Flesh Gordon* was and said condescendingly, 'It had some rather good special effects ...'. Well, I disagree on both counts—I thought it had a very good script and some really stunning photography and special effects (Harold Ziehm and others deserve more credit than 'rather good' I think). What a delightful parody of the *Flash Gordon* films this was; I shall look forward to its sequel, *The Perils of Flesh.*

[Published in Film Review, *1974. As far as I can gather the sequel was never made!]*

Awards for Anderson

Lindsay Anderson's mildly iconoclastic film, *O Lucky Man!*, dealing with the cyclical nature of success and failure, must surely be heading for many awards. Alan Price's music, Ondříček's photography, Anderson's direction, and Miriam Brickman's casting are so much more than adequate. One could criticise the rather lazy style of film editing, the long lap dissolves, but so many other features of the film more than compensate. Another success for the *If....* team.

[Published in Film Review, *1973.]*

A Great Chiller

Having now seen Hitchcock's chiller *The Birds* twice, I doubt if ever there'll be a film quite like it again. We have had *Willard*, *Frogs*, and *They Only Kill Their Masters* (films which hint at rats, frogs, and dogs revolting against man) but for my money, if you want ice massaged on your nerves, *The Birds* is the film. Full marks to Lawrence Hampton for his effects which were all too real, and, of course, Ray Berwick for training the birds. Made some ten years ago, this film will never cease to chill my blood.

[Published in Film Review, *1973.]*

Technology on the Screen

Westworld, I see, was directed and written by surgeon Michael Crichton—and it shows. The attention to detail and production design was excellent and he coaxed very good performances from Richard Benjamin, Yul Brynner, and James Brolin. Comparison with *2001: A Space Odyssey* I think is valid—this latest film showing yet again the dangers very advanced technology can bring, especially in the computer and robot fields.

[Published in Film Review, *1973.]*

Superfilm

If I had to assemble a crew and cast for my ideal film, I would choose the following:

Director: Roman (*Macbeth*) Polanski; Producer: Carlo (*Doctor Zhivago*) Ponti; Production Designer: Ken (any 007 film) Adam; Screenwriter: Paul (*Poseidon Adventure*) Gallico; Cinematographer: Geoffrey (*2001: A Space Odyssey*) Unsworth; Music score: John (007) Barry and Henry (*Pink Panther*) Mancini; Title Design: Saul (*Spartacus*) Bass; Make-up Design: Dick (*Exorcist*) Smith; Costumes: Edith (*Carpetbaggers*) Head. The key actors: Jon Finch, Goldie Hawn, Dustin Hoffman, Christopher Jones, Julie Christie, Ralph Richardson, Christopher Gable. What the film would be about and what its title would be, I'm not so sure!

[Published in Film Review, *date uncertain—probably early 1970s. I cringe at the letter and these choices now, especially of actors, but*

this is what I wrote at the time. The free cinema tickets were very welcome anyway!]

My Favourite Film

I have always felt it a rather pointless exercise to name one's favourite film. After all, who knows what films one may encounter in future that may change one's mind? To date I'm certain that of all the films I've seen so far, *Cinema Paradiso* is the one I would save if the tide threatened to wash away all my selected favourites from that mythical desert island.

Cinema Paradiso (1988)
Cinema Paradiso (Director's Cut, 2002)
Writer/Dir.: Giuseppe Tornatore
[The film is in Italian, with English subtitles.]

Synopsis

The film opens in Rome with Salvatore Di Vita (Jacques Perrin), a successful film director, receiving a message from his mother in Sicily that someone called Alfredo has died and that his funeral is the following afternoon. The message is relayed to him by a young woman, one of a succession of girlfriends that Salvatore has had in the recent past. The shock of this news prompts a flashback to Salvatore's youth in Sicily in the 1940s, where he used to be nicknamed Toto (played by a young Salvatore Cascio). Toto's father was largely absent from his life as he was fighting on the Russian Front. Toto was befriended by the local projectionist, Alfredo (Philippe Noiret), at the town's cinema, the Cinema Paradiso. Toto was fascinated and obsessed with films from an early age, from how the projector was operated to the 'in situ' censorship of any scene of intimacy, including kissing, which was censored by the local priest previewing them. This was done by him ringing a bell every time such a scene appeared, then Alfredo would cut out the offending shot.

Alfredo became a father figure to Toto as the child's father was absent from his life. One night a fire broke out in the cinema and Alfredo is blinded. However, the cinema is rebuilt and Toto becomes the new projectionist. The film now jumps ten years and Toto is now

41

played by Marco Leonardi. He begins making amateur films and starts to fall in love with a beautiful girl called Elena. Alfredo feels that Toto is wasting his time in this small town and that he should leave to make a better life for himself. Although Toto and Elena had made tentative plans to meet, a misunderstanding led Toto to leave Sicily without contacting her.

The film ends with Toto (now Salvatore) returning home to attend Alfredo's funeral, where he discovers that Alfredo had left him a gift: a reel of film containing all the assembled shots of actors kissing. A kissing montage which lasts several minutes is one of the most endearing and enduring scenes in the film, notably for the expressions on Salvatore's face as he watches the screen. Alfredo may have left the reel to remind Salvatore of the importance of love and to tell him to look for happiness in his personal life.

Critique

The film may ostensibly be seen as a homage to cinema, but in fact its themes are far more universal than that. There is the theme of isolation—Toto was isolated from his father at an early age; he isolated himself from his family and his mother and, in a way, has isolated, or 'insulated' himself from love. His mother tellingly says to him, *'When I call you, a different woman always answers. But so far, I've never heard one voice that really loves you.'* Only a mother's intuition could know these things, and perhaps only a caring mother would be brave enough to say it. Salvatore's return to Sicily to see his family has taken him thirty years. He tells his mother that it only takes an hour to fly from Rome to Sicily. She replies: *'You shouldn't tell me that now. Not after all these years.'*

There is too the theme of love and missed opportunity. The missed opportunity of loving Elena (who had married one of his friends in his absence), the love between Toto and Alfredo that was as strong, if not stronger, than his own father could have provided. Some have stated that the film is overly sentimental, syrupy, and saccharine. I can see their point of view but on thinking carefully about the final montage, and Salvatore's face on seeing the cinematic depictions of love, kissing, embraces—these are things that he himself could have enjoyed but didn't. It is one of those endings which are truly joyful and sad at the same time. Is Salvatore's 'happiness' true or delusional? Few films have that kind of ending. Throughout, Ennio Morricone's score is everywhere apt, but until the very end scene, it has a muted and slightly restrained quality about it. During the last scene, the theme fully blossoms into its powerful, completely unrestrained climax. The music is, in effect, finally giving you permission to weep. And you will. Whether with joy, sadness, or both is unpredictable, but weep you will.

Awards
Cinema Paradiso was voted Best Film of the Decade in a *Guardian* poll where readers voted for the best film made from 1980–1993.

It won an Oscar for the Best Foreign Film Award in 1990.

It won a BAFTA for Best Film not in the English Language, Best Original Score, Best Original Screenplay, Best Actor (Philippe Noiret), and Best Supporting Actor (Salvatore Cascio) in 1991.

The Cinematography, Costume Design, Direction, Make-up, and Editing were nominated for BAFTAs.

It also won, or was nominated for, a host of other international awards.

Film Critics I Admired

Barry Norman (1933–2017)

Barry Norman was the son of Leslie Norman, a film director who directed *The Cruel Sea* (1954) and *Dunkirk* (1958), a superior film in my opinion to the recent 2017 version. He was a journalist and contributor to the cartoon *Flook* and presented a weekly film review programme on BBC One from 1972–1998. He had a jovial and avuncular personality, a sort of 'uncle' figure whom one could imagine advising you on how best to spend your pocket money at the cinema whilst throwing in some *bon mots* on the quality of the acting, plot, or direction. He did this with an enormous sense of fun and understated humour and I eagerly awaited his pronouncements on the latest releases.

One I recall was on the film *Mame*, made in 1974, and starring Lucille Ball. Whenever Miss Ball's face was in close-up, the photography became extremely soft-focus, presumably to hide her wrinkles (though she was only sixty-three at the time). Here, as far as I can recall them, were Barry's comments:

> *'Miss Ball is photographed through so many layers of gauze to hide her wrinkles, there are times when she begins to look like the ghost of Danny La Rue.'*

I was having a cup of tea at the time and I believe I aerosolised most of it over my mother's best carpet.

Another comment on a Western (whose name I can't recall):

> *'This is a good old-fashioned Western, where the goodies are goodies and the baddies are baddies. None of your psychological nonsense about baddies being baddies because they were taken off the breast too soon.'*

I wish I could recall others but they're legion. I miss Barry and his down-to-earth approach to cinema. In 2007, he marketed his own brand of pickled onions, a business now being managed by his two daughters.

Pauline Kael (1919–2001)

Pauline Kael was an American film critic who mainly wrote for *The New Yorker*. Witty, biting, highly opinionated, and sharply focused reviews, her opinions were often contrary to those of her contemporaries. She was one of the most influential (and probably feared) film critics of her day. She authored at least fourteen books of film criticism, including *I Lost It at the Movies*. Many directors and actors who became the butt of her reviews would probably posit the view that it was her temper she lost at the movies.

Her review of *Ryan's Daughter* (1970):

> *'Gush made respectable by millions of dollars tastefully wasted ...'*

This review (and others) sent David Lean into a deep depression. He didn't make another film for fourteen years (*Passage to India* [1984], his last film). If you watch an interview with Lean and Melvyn Bragg on YouTube, you'll appreciate the effects a critic's words can have on a director, including someone as tough and obstinate as David Lean. If someone tells you often enough that you've produced rubbish you tend to believe it, he says.

The Lean/Bragg interview:
https://www.youtube.com/watch?v=QvB-u7vVZus

Pauline Kael's other books include:

Kiss Kiss Bang Bang (1966)

Going Steady (1969)

The Citizen Kane Book (1971)

Deeper into Movies (1973)

Reeling (1976)

When the Lights Go Down (1980)

5001 Nights at the Movies (1982, revised in 1984 and 1991)

Taking It All In (1984)

State of the Art (1985)

Hooked (1989)

Movie Love (1991)

For Keeps (1994)

Raising Kane, and Other Essays (1996)

Dilys Powell (1901–1995)

Dilys Powell, CBE was an English journalist who wrote for *The Sunday Times* for over fifty years and was the author of several books on films and on her travels in Greece. Powell was noted for her receptiveness to cultural change in the cinema, and she coined many classic phrases about films and actors. Dirk Bogarde had much correspondence with Dilys Powell, recognising the 'activating' effect cinema had on both of them, e.g.

> '... the wondrous thing is that the instant one speaks of the cinema you are instantly alive and alert ... the cinema is your 'fix'. I know that. I recognise that ... I revelled. Perhaps that's the only real time that I come alive.'
> (from *Ever, Dirk: The Bogarde Letters*)

One got the impression that Miss Powell was so polite and well-mannered that to even gently criticise a film would almost cause her physical pain. If she didn't like a film, you were made well aware of that fact, backed up by sound evidence. In 1991 the *Dilys Powell Award for Excellence in Film* was established by the London Critics' Circle (criticscircle.org.uk). The first recipient was Dirk Bogarde and at the time of writing (2019), the latest was Pedro Almodóvar. She has published collections of her film reviews, notably, *The Golden Screen: Fifty Years of Film,* covering films from 1939–1988.

George Melly (1926–2007)

George Heywood Melly was an English critic and blues singer, writer, and lecturer. From 1965–1973 he was a film and television critic for *The Observer* and lectured on art history, with an emphasis on surrealism. He wrote several screenplays, including one based on Kingsley Amis's novel, *Take A Girl Like You.*

Sadly I can't recall or locate any of his published film reviews but I do remember writing to him at *The Observer* in the 1970s asking him who wrote the play on which a film I'd enjoyed, *The Ruling Class,* was based. In that pre-digital age there was no internet or Google to consult and unless one had a good memory for the credits, or a good film magazine to consult, one was stymied. Several weeks later, a letter came from Mr Melly stating that the playwright was one Peter Barnes. He added that 'it was a very enjoyable film wasn't it?' and ended with an enormous flourish of a signature which took up half a page of the letter! I wish I'd kept it now.

Manhattan skyline, 1990

Noguchi Cube, New York

The Dakota Building, New York

UN and Chrysler Buildings, New York

51

Superdome, New Orleans

Outside Café du Monde, New Orleans

Monument to the Discoveries, Lisbon

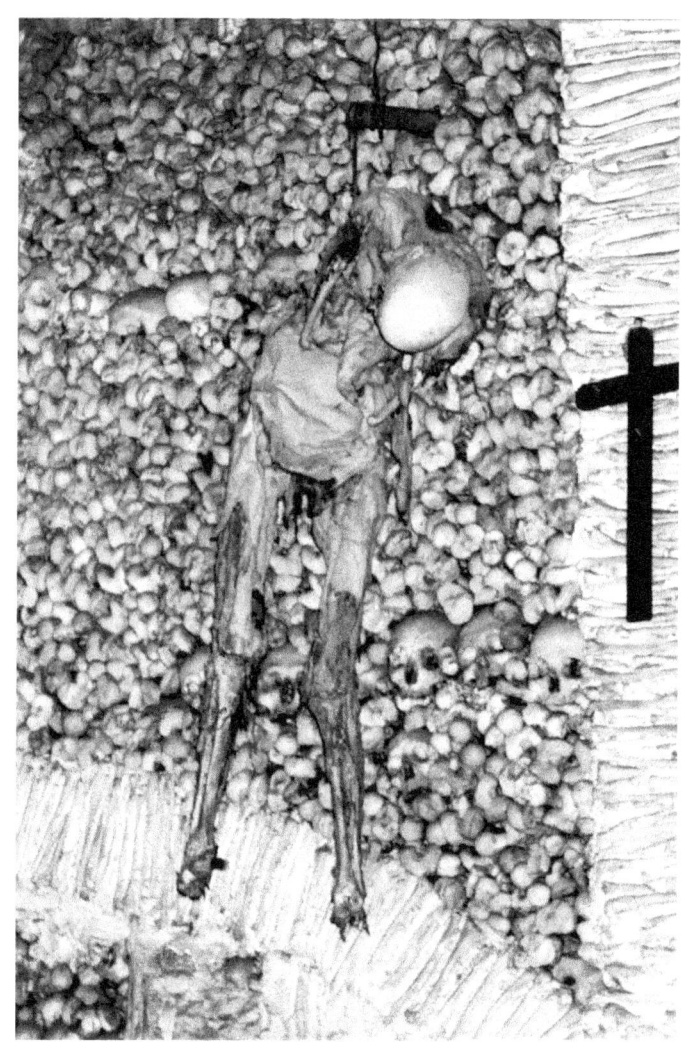

Capela dos Ossos, Évora, Portugal

Évora, Portugal

Berlenga Fortress and Monastery, Portugal

55

Marigot Bay, St Lucia

Prague Castle Guard

Ölüdeniz, Turkey

Pamukkale, Turkey

58

The author, Richard Owen, in 1989

Credit Where Credit's Due

What is a best boy anyway—or what do those film credits mean?

Few people stay to watch the end credits of a film but even if they do, they whizz past too quickly or mystify one with terms such as 'best boy', 'gaffer', or 'key grip'. Of all these terms, the 'best boy' has probably attracted most attention and intrigue. Is he perhaps the director's boyfriend and what makes him 'best' as opposed to 'quite good' or 'barely adequate'? Could he possibly be involved in photographing the 'best man' at a wedding scene? Is there a 'best girl', 'worst boy' … or … the mind boggles at the possibilities. The *Airplane* series of films even extended their comedic flair into the credits; in the first of the series the 'best boy' credit is then followed by 'Worst boy: Adolf Hitler'.

These are not the only credits: what is a script supervisor, Foley artist, focus puller, executive producer, the difference between an art director and a production designer? Why does the director of photography often have BSC or ASC after their name or the editor ACE after theirs? Does the latter denote a really good (i.e. 'ace') film editor? I shall try and answer some of these questions with selected examples and discuss some of the work of the best 'backroom boys' whose work you have probably either already seen, or heard of.

Best Boy

There are two types of best boy: *best boy electrical* and *best boy grip*. The best boy electrical is the assistant to the 'gaffer' who is in charge of electricians on the set. In effect, the 'best boy electrical' is the assistant electrician. The 'best boy grip' is assistant to the 'key grip' who is in charge of rigging and lighting. The 'best boy', whether electrical or grip, acts as the foreman for his department. Women also now perform these duties and the term 'best girl' has been seen in film credits.

This still leaves the thorny question of why the adjective 'best' precedes 'boy' or 'girl'. No one really seems to know, but the title is believed to have arisen when the chief electrician (or 'gaffer') went round other departments asking if they could 'lend him their best boy'. Within the confines of a film set, no one would presumably bat an eyelid at such a question. In any other context however, eyebrows may well be raised, and in this very PC climate, the possibility of some sort of official, even legal, complaint cannot be ruled out! One can imagine the Twitter feed now: # *yes, but I really did mean assistant electrician, your Lordship.*

Script Supervisor

When I first saw this term, I had envisaged a sort of cinematic equivalent to a theatrical 'prompt' person, who would correct an actor if they strayed away from the written word. They may well take on this role, although I imagine the director, or even the actor him or herself, would realise their mistake(s). However, the older term for a *script supervisor* was the more self-explanatory 'continuity supervisor' and sometimes, one may see the term 'script girl' used in older films. No doubt the latter is seen as rather sexist these days but moreover, it doesn't really clarify the role. The *script supervisor* oversees the continuity of wardrobe, props, set dressing, hair and make-up, and actions of the actors during a scene. Films are very rarely shot in the sequences shown in the script and thus this role is a vital one. The notes recorded during the shooting help the editor cut the scene in post-production and the script supervisor is the writer and editor's representative on set and the right-hand aide to both director and director of photography.

Excellent though script supervisors may be, almost *every* film ends up with a host of goofs and continuity errors. For those who love to know about these things visit imdb.com (International Movie Database.com) where, along with stars, crew, plot summary, and locations, you will find a listing of goofs, continuity errors, and trivia.

Foley Artist

The Foley artist, named after sound-effects artist Jack Foley (1891–1967), is involved in the reproduction of everyday sounds that are added to film, video, and other media, post-production. These involve footsteps, squeaky doors, breaking glass, ticking clocks, etc.

During the filming of *Psycho*, the Foley artist found that the best sound effects to simulate flesh being stabbed in the infamous shower scene were produced by stabbing a casaba melon. Some twenty different types of melon were tried before Hitch declared himself satisfied with the sound. Even that sound was then blended with a sirloin steak being stabbed! One wonders whether the audience would have noticed what sound was made, what with Bernard Herrmann's screechy score and Janet Leigh's screams in the background. Hitch had originally intended to film the shower scene without any music, but Herrmann said that he had already prepared some music and would Hitch care to listen to it? He did—and the rest is cinema history.

A recent documentary film, concerning itself entirely with the shower scene in *Psycho*, was released in 2017, called *78/52*. The shower scene contained seventy-eight camera set-ups and fifty-two editorial cuts, hence the film's title.

Art Director/Production Designer

Art directors translate the production designer's vision for the film and are responsible for the department's budget and work schedules and report to the production designer. Production designers are involved with the creation and organisation of the physical world surrounding a film story.

Previously (and often subsequently) the people with the same responsibilities were called art directors. The term production designer is said to have been invented by William Cameron Menzies, although some suggest that it was coined for him by producer David Selznick (1902–1965) for Menzies' outstanding contribution to *Gone with the Wind* (1939). The title was apparently created to honour the fact that Menzies had done so much more than just supervise the set construction but coordinated every phase of the production that was not covered by dialogue or action. This included very detailed storyboarding which even included the POV (point of view) of the camera for each scene. However the IMDb database probably incorrectly lists Menzies as a production designer in a 1918 film (*The Naulahka*), although other sources such as *Halliwell's Film, DVD & Video Guide 2007* cite him as art director. I would tend to believe the latter source. The Oscar for Best Art Direction award remained thus called, from 1928 until 2012 when it was changed to Oscar for Best Production Design.

Director of Photography

Hopefully the reader will not think I'm insulting their intelligence by explaining what a director of photography does. After all, as everyone knows, he's the guy (or girl) behind the camera, right? Well, only rarely would a DOP or DP (Director of Photography) be found behind the camera, unless checking a shot or perhaps if they worked on a small independent production, where they would be the camera operator too (see later section). DPs are basically heads of department on film productions and are intimately involved with two key aspects: recording the images and lighting them. In fact, you may sometimes see the terms *lighting cameraman* or *cinematographer* used; these personnel are generally freelance and they can often choose how they wish to be credited. DPs must discover the 'photographic heart' of a screenplay, often using still photographs, paintings, and other films or media. They create the desired look of a film, using lighting, filters, framing, camera movement, or film processing techniques (if not using digital recording). They often agree the 'colour palette' of a film (e.g. brash primary colours, or muted sepia tones, etc.) with the director and production and costume designer.

You will often see the letters BSC or ASC after a DP's name. BSC stands for the British Society of Cinematographers, established in 1949. ASC stands for the American Society of Cinematographers, established in 1919. Many others abound: e.g. CSC: Canadian Society of Cinematographers, DFF: Dansk Filmfotograf Forbund (Danish Society of Cinematographers), etc. Usually these accreditations are by invitation only, not by examinations; it is an honorary accreditation.

Some cinematographers, e.g. Roger (*Skyfall, Blade Runner 2049*, etc.) Deakins has been accredited by both UK and US societies and can add BSC and ASC after his name. Does it make any difference to the quality of their photography? No, but as a freelance person it probably means they can command a much higher fee!

I emailed the BSC asking them which film was the first to mention the credit 'Director of Photography' after a cinematographer's name. What an interesting question, came the reply, we've no idea! They got one of their esteemed members, Phil Meheux (who was DP on Bond films *Casino Royale, Goldenyeye*, and about fifty-three other films) to do some research on it. The earliest screen credit he could find with the words Director of Photography (Joseph Valentine) was given on the Universal Picture *One Hundred Men and a Girl* in 1936, starring Deanna Durbin and Leopold Stokowski. I've not seen the film, but it does rather sound as if it could be one of those films one might find in a backstreet Soho shop. (It isn't!)

Focus Puller/Camera Operator/2nd Camera Assistant

The *Focus puller* (or *1st Camera Assistant*) adjusts the camera lens (or 'pulls focus') to follow the action on set. The *Camera Operator* is responsible for all aspects of camera preparation and operation and yes, *this* is the guy behind the camera! The *2nd Camera Assistant* provides camera maintenance and film or tape stock control. They load and unload camera magazines and ensure correct stock is used (if using film). They change camera batteries and provide other accessories if needed. They are also responsible for the clapperboard and may take the daily rushes to the processing lab (if film rather than digital media is being used).

Film Editor

Well, this title *is* self-explanatory, but there are some aspects which may not be. Some editors have the letters ACE (American Cinema Editors) or GBFTE (Guild of British Film and Television Editors) after their names, founded in 1950 and 1966, respectively. The editor works closely with the director to craft the finished film; editing is the cinematic equivalent of grammar and punctuation in prose. Editors work in an edit suite for long hours and may also be responsible for synchronising the soundtrack with the images. On big productions they run a team of assistants and trainees. Some of the greatest directors were editors previously: David Lean, Alfred Hitchcock, and many others. Hitchcock's wife, Alma Reville, was an editor and often advised Hitch on productions he was working on. The editor is probably the last and only person who can salvage or amend a film, once it has been shot. It was Alma that noticed, during a preview of *Psycho*, that after Janet Leigh had 'died' in the shower, a close-up of her eye showed that she had blinked. The scene was re-shot.

When Hitch told Alma that he was thinking of killing off Janet Leigh halfway through *Psycho*, she allegedly replied, 'No, don't do that; kill her off a third of the way through.' Whether true or not, one of the biggest shocks for cinema audiences watching *Psycho* was probably not the shower scene per se, but that a major star had been killed off 45 minutes into a film lasting 109 minutes.

Executive Producer vs. Producer

The role of the *executive producer* is to oversee the work of the *producer* on behalf of the studio, financiers, or distributors. This ensures the film is completed on time, within budget, and to agreed artistic and technical standards. (This does not always happen though.) The *producer* is involved in turning story ideas into profitable films by acquiring film rights, pulling together a creative and talented cast and crew, being responsible for all aspects of the film's production, and marketing the film to distributors and media. The initials p.g.a (Producer's Guild of America) often follows a producer's name in the US.

A Few of the Best Cinematographers and Designers

Cinematographers

Freddie (Frederick) Young, OBE, BSC (1902–1998)

Frederick Archibald Young (often credited as F. A. Young) was a British cinematographer who is probably best known for his work on David Lean's films, three of which won him Academy Awards for Best Cinematography. A small selection of films lensed by Young, with their awards or nominations, is listed below:

Inn of the Sixth Happiness (1958)
Lawrence of Arabia (1962), AA (Academy Award or Oscar)
Doctor Zhivago (1965), AA
You Only Live Twice (1967)
Ryan's Daughter (1970), AA
Nicholas and Alexandra (1971), AAN (Academy Award Nomination)
The Tamarind Seed (1974)

Allegedly, *Lawrence of Arabia* was the first film to successfully photograph a mirage. For the shot where Omar Sharif makes an appearance on his camel from several miles away and gradually approaches the camera, a 400 mm lens was used and specially created just for this scene. The lens was never used again for any film. Young was the only cinematographer who agreed to light the gigantic *You Only Live Twice* volcano set, discussed in more detail under Ken Adam's section.

Geoffrey Unsworth, OBE, BSC (1914–1978)

Geoffrey Gilyard Unsworth was a British cinematographer who worked on nearly ninety feature films over more than forty years. He is best known for his work on films such as Stanley Kubrick's *2001: A Space Odyssey*, Bob Fosse's *Cabaret*, and Richard Donner's *Superman*.

A small selection of films photographed by Geoffrey Unsworth include:

Becket (1964), AA, BAFTA
2001: A Space Odyssey (1968)
Cabaret (1972), AA, BAFTA
Murder on the Orient Express (1974), AAN
A Bridge Too Far (1977), BAFTA
Superman (1978)
Tess (1978), AA, BAFTA*

*Sadly, Geoffrey Unsworth died on the set whilst filming Roman Polanski's *Tess* in 1978. The cinematography was completed by Ghislain Cloquet who accepted the Oscar on his behalf.

Jack Cardiff, OBE, BSC (1914–2009)

Jack Cardiff was a British cinematographer, director, and photographer. His career spanned the development of cinema from silent film through early experimentation with Technicolor to filmmaking more than fifty years later. He was best known for his influential colour cinematography for directors like Powell and Pressburger (*A Matter of Life and Death*), Huston (*The African Queen*), and Hitchcock (*Under Capricorn*). In the film *A Matter of Life and Death* (1946), his innovative use of colour and black and white in the same film depicted Heaven (or The Other World) in black and white whilst scenes down on Earth were in Technicolor. In fact, the black and white scenes were partially developed Technicolor, giving them a strange pearly hue. A small selection of films photographed by Jack Cardiff include:

A Matter of Life and Death (1946)
Black Narcissus (1947), AA
The Red Shoes (1948)
The Vikings (1958)
Death on The Nile (1978)

Production Designers

Ken Adam (born Claus Adam), OBE (1921–2016)

A German-born art director who came to the UK after the rise of Nazi Germany. He was only one of three German-born pilots who served in the RAF during World War II. He trained under William Cameron Menzies. Some films designed by Ken Adam include:

Dr. Strangelove (1962)
Dr. No (1962)
Goldfinger (1964)
You Only Live Twice (1967)
Diamonds Are Forever (1971)
Live and Let Die (1973)
The Spy Who Loved Me (1977)
Moonraker (1979)
Chitty Chitty Bang Bang (1968)
Barry Lyndon (1975), AA
The Madness of King George (1994), AA

As you can see, he was long a stalwart of the Bond films. I can recall Sean Connery stating in an interview that it was a disgrace that some of the Bond set designs hadn't even been nominated for a design Oscar, let alone won one. He thought this may have been something to do with the fact that Adam was credited as a production designer rather than an art director (the Oscar at that time was for Art Direction) but personally, I don't think this seems likely. The two Oscars he did win, for *Barry Lyndon* and *The Madness of King George,* to my mind, did not display his creative best since many of the scenes were outdoors or didn't employ constructed sets, but buildings already in existence.

In *Dr. Strangelove,* the War Room set is a triumph of production design, since, in an overhead shot, the room resembles a remarkable similarity to the crest of a mushroom cloud, and is very apt since the film is about the atomic bomb. Indeed, the film's subtitle is: *How I Learned to Stop Worrying and Love the Bomb.* When Ronald Reagan became President, after seeing *Dr. Strangelove,* he was very keen to visit the Pentagon War Room. He was very disappointed that it did not in the least resemble the one in *Dr. Strangelove!* One of the most memorable lines in the film is when Peter Sellers (playing a US president) shouts at his colleagues, 'Gentlemen, stop arguing, this is a WAR ROOM!' One wonders if Reagan had occasion to shout a similar line to his colleagues in the real War Room.

In *Goldfinger,* we see Ken Adam's impression of what the inside of Fort Knox would look like. The production weren't allowed permission to enter it and the area is heavily guarded for around two miles surrounding the building; loudspeakers constantly warn you to leave the area. When J. Edgar Hoover, then head of the FBI, saw the film it was rumoured that he thought someone had let Ken Adam in to sketch the interior. Adam had however been allowed to enter the Bank of England's vaults to see how they stored their gold ingots. They were stored rather low and seemed a bit underwhelming so in the set, he stocked them higher to make them more impressive. After the film was released, 200 irate filmgoers wrote to United Artists demanding to know why a British crew would be allowed to film in Fort Knox, when their own President couldn't get in. Adam's 'vision' of Fort Knox's interior was not far off the mark I think! He certainly fulfilled his vision of constructing a 'cathedral of gold'.

Another truly impressive set design was the volcano interior used for rocket launches in the Bond film *You Only Live Twice.* It wasn't in Fleming's novel but when Roald Dahl is on scriptwriting duty you just know he's going to let his imagination leap high. At the time (1967), this set was the most expensive ever constructed at $1 million (today this would be about $7 million or £6.6m). In a radio interview, Ken Adam said he came out in a nervous rash with the strain of his responsibility; his doctor prescribed Valium and the rash soon went. Ken Adam still had nightmares wondering how they were going to light it and Freddie Young was the only cinematographer they could find who was willing to do so. They used every single light the studio had and yet had to borrow more from European studios. The set was so vast it would take a minute of screen time for a character to walk across it.

John Box, OBE (1920–2005)

John Allan Hyatt Box was a British production designer and art director. During his career he won an Oscar for Best Art Direction on four occasions and the equivalent BAFTA three times. Throughout his career he gained a reputation for recreating exotic locations in rather more mundane surroundings and even created a walled Chinese city in Snowdonia. Some films designed by John Box include:

Inn of the Sixth Happiness (1958)
Lawrence of Arabia (1962), AA
Doctor Zhivago (1965), AA
A Man for All Seasons (1966), BAFTA
Oliver (1968), AA
Nicholas and Alexandra (1971), AA
The Great Gatsby (1974), AA
A Passage to India (1984), AAN

In the book *A Snowdonia Childhood: A London Boy Growing Up in Beddgelert* by Richard J. Bernard, the author mentions moving from London to Beddgelert and The Goat Hotel, which had just been bought by his parents in 1957. In 1958, *The Inn of the Sixth Happiness* was being filmed at Nantmor, near Beddgelert. Most of the crew stayed at the hotel, including John Box, the production designer. His room was adjacent to Richard's and he once heard John on the phone, ordering another 10,000 feet of scaffolding to build The Great Wall of China. He also heard him tell his father that 'it was possible to find the whole world in North Wales'. Well, after all, it has, in various films, stood in for China (*The Most Dangerous Man in the World*), Scotland (Polanski's *Macbeth*), Pakistan (the Khyber Pass in *Carry On Up The Khyber!*), and countless others.

John Box returned to North Wales in 1995 and was designer on the film *First Knight* starring Sean Connery and Richard Gere, filmed near Trawsfynydd, Harlech, and Blaenau Ffestiniog. The premiere was held at The Coliseum cinema in Porthmadog, a beautiful 1930s Art Deco building, now sadly demolished and still awaiting a buyer to replace a much missed building in the town.

Stephen Grimes (1927–1988)

Stephen B. Grimes was an English production designer and art director and won one Oscar for *Out of Africa* (1985) and appeared briefly as an official in the film. He was nominated for two other Oscars for *The Night of The Iguana* (1962) and *The Way We Were* (1973) and received a BAFTA nomination for *Ryan's Daughter* (1970) where a whole village (Kirrary) was built from scratch, well before the era of CGI (computer generated images).

William Cameron Menzies (1896–1957)

William Cameron Menzies was an American production designer and art director. He is always cited as being the first production designer, after his work on *Gone with the Wind* (1939). He also directed twenty-four films (according to IMDb), although strangely, he is uncredited on five of them. He won the first Oscar for Best Art Direction on two films, *The Dove* and *The Tempest*, both made in 1928. Some of his best design work includes *Gone with the Wind*, for which he received an honorary Oscar for 'outstanding achievement in the use of color for the enhancement of dramatic mood in the production of *Gone with the Wind*'.

He also directed the burning of Atlanta sequence and also reshot the Salvador Dalí dream sequence in Hitchcock's film *Spellbound*. He is credited as associate producer on *Around the World in Eighty Days*; his protégé Ken Adam was art director on that film, but curiously, his name was stated as Ken Adams not Adam.

Title Designers

Until around the late 1950s titles were rather plain and boring, words projected onto a plain background, just something to let you know who was in the film, who photographed it and directed it, etc. Few people cared. However, with the advent of title designers like Saul Bass, titles could become vehicles which hinted at the tone of a film, whether comedy, drama, or musical; the choice of font and font size mattered, the background and the editing mattered. They were meant to bring you in line with the key themes of the film; something to jolt you from the bad day you'd had and not something to idly watch as you munched your popcorn or crisps. They were, in effect, a sort of cinematic poster.

In the early films the person responsible for the titles was uncredited. Now that the title sequence has arrived, the title designer's name is often on the opening credits and he (or she) often gets a stand-alone credit, unhampered by other people's names. There is even a video channel called *Forget the Film, Watch the Titles* where you can watch over 200 film title sequences. Many films today have no opening title sequences; a great pity in my opinion. Here are some of the most notable technicians of the art:

Saul Bass (1921–1996)

Saul Bass was a well-known American film title designer, having designed the title sequences of over fifty films, including *Psycho*, *Vertigo*, *North by Northwest*, *Cape Fear*, and *It's a Mad, Mad,*

Mad, Mad World. He worked initially in advertising as a graphic artist. He created logos for a huge number of branded products and airlines, many of which are still in use today. These include Quaker Oats, Kleenex, Continental Airlines, Minolta, AT&T, US Mail, General Foods, and a host of others. Subsequently he directed a film about an ant invasion called *Phase IV*, although this was not a huge critical success. He storyboarded the shower scene in *Psycho* and (allegedly) directed it. Hitchcock said he had to reshoot it, but Bass disagreed.

Whilst on holiday in Florida in 1990, I visited Universal Studios where they had a visitor exhibit called *Alfred Hitchcock: The Art of Making Movies* and they showed the camera set-ups and angles used for the shower scene in *Psycho*; a volunteer in a plastic cape allowed water to be sprayed on him while the shower cubicle slowly revolved so that a number of angles could be covered by an array of cameras peeking over the cubicle's top. On my return home I wrote to Universal Studios and asked if they could shed light on who actually directed the shower scene—Bass or Hitchcock? I received a letter from Susan Lustig, the Show Producer for the exhibit. Excerpts of her letter are shown below:

> *'I do wish I could shed some light on your question as to who directed the shower scene in* Psycho. *Mr. Hitchcock is quoted in the Francois Truffaut book [*Hitchcock/Truffaut*] that he asked Mr. Bass, due to a bout of flu, to shoot the scene of the detective falling down the steps for him. Mr Hitchcock further states that this scene was the only scene Mr. Bass shot. Mr. Hitchcock said that he had to reshoot this scene anyway since it was not what he wanted.*
>
> *I did see an interview with Mr. Bass claiming that he shot the [shower] scene. I suppose my personal conclusion, no matter who actually sat in the director's chair, is that it was, after all is said and done, Mr. Hitchcock's film. He always storyboarded practically every shot of his films, so knew exactly what was going to appear in the dailies. Mr. Hitchcock hated surprises. Also, from his early filmmaking days, he got into the habit of shooting exactly to these boards so the editor*

had to edit to Mr. Hitchcock's vision ... no coverage was provided therefore no creative license on the part of the editor could be taken. I also know Mr. Hitchcock was definitely there for the filming of this landmark scene, so I cannot imagine him letting go of creative control, and that is, I trust, the basis for your question ... I'm sorry I must give you a gray answer rather than one that is black and white but again, I do appreciate your interest.

Susan J. Lustig
Show Producer

I tend to think that it was Hitch who shot the shower scene after all. Surely cast and crew members would by now have gone to print to say otherwise if that was not the case, either after the film's release or after Hitchcock's death in 1980? However, I'm intrigued by Ms Lustig's assertion that she 'knew Hitchcock was definitely there for ... this landmark scene' yet apologises for her 'gray answer'. After reading a book co-written by Jennifer Bass (Bass's daughter) and Pat Kirkham (*Saul Bass: A Life in Film and Design*), Bass maintains that Hitchcock was certainly present for the shower scene but let Bass direct it. On seeing the resulting sequence, Hitch insisted on two additional inserts. However in the Truffaut interview cited in the book *Hitchcock/Truffaut*, Hitchcock stated that Bass only filmed the sequence where the detective Arbogast (Martin Balsam) falls down the stairs. Why Hitch had what ostensibly seems to be selective amnesia remains a mystery.

I'm going to briefly describe two of Saul Bass's impressive title sequences, the ones for *Vertigo* and *North by Northwest*.

Vertigo (1958)

The themes of *Vertigo* involve obsession, anxiety, acrophobia (fear of heights), identity, and voyeurism. The title sequence begins with a close-up of a woman's face, nervous, twitchy, and looking left and right periodically with her eyes. The camera then zooms in on her eye, now bathed in a reddish light, and enters ever deeper, until her pupil morphs into spirals which keep changing shape and colour, circling round and round without pause. This conveys well the theme of obsession since obsessions are about circling back to the same moment, again and again and again ... Some spirals also resemble a section of Kim Novak's (the female lead's) hair and one scene in the film involves a close-up of her hair tied into a bun. The music too has many repetitive chords and never actually comes to a resolution, reinforcing the nature of obsession. Finally, the camera zooms out of the eye and the director's name emerges from a very small point within the pupil to fill the screen.

We have, in a way, been on a journey into this woman's mind and out of it. Make no mistake, *Vertigo* is a psychological thriller. Hitch took about two hours to explore these themes; Saul Bass did all of these in about three minutes! The spirals are called Lissajous spirals based on the work of a physicist, Jules Antoine Lissajous, and Bass was aided by computer animator John Whitney (uncredited) in creating them; perhaps the very first computer-animated title sequence?

North by Northwest (1959)

To a pounding Bernard Herrmann score, the construction of a blue grid starts to appear against a green background. As the music continues, the credits start appearing within the grid. However, the titles and the grid are tilted, not in any direction, but on a north by northwest slant, reinforcing the film's title and a plot point within the film. About half way through the title sequence, the grid fades unobtrusively and then we are left with a real-life 'grid'—rows of windows outside a huge building, the United Nations building in New York. The credits now appear with the confines of the glass and steel 'grid' of the building. The building is central to the plot since the first murder occurs within it, and the chief suspect (Cary Grant) works in it. As we zoom away from the building, streams of people are walking away from it towards a bus, some people enter it, and it pulls away before the last passenger can board, Alfred Hitchcock himself—neatly timed as his name appears on screen. This title sequence may have been the first to use 'kinetic typography', where the letters move about on the screen rather than being projected onto it.

Maurice Binder (1925–1991)

Maurice Binder was an American film title designer, best known for his work on fourteen James Bond films, including the first, *Dr. No*, in 1962. Binder also created the signature gun barrel sequence for the opening titles of the films, reprised in many forms since then. His signature themes, especially for the Bond films, involved silhouettes: women dancing, trampolining, somersaulting, swimming, clambering over gun barrels, caressing jewellery … Whatever the film was like, one could be assured of a stylish start if it had a Maurice Binder title sequence. Some might even say that the titles were, in fact, better than the films themselves. In essence, they were, perhaps, the first pop videos.

Daniel (Danny) Kleinman (1955–)

Daniel Kleinman is a British commercial and video director who also designed every title sequence for the Bond films since *Goldeneye* (1995), with the exception of *Quantum of Solace* (2008). He returned to design the title sequences for *Skyfall* (2012) and *Spectre* (2015). The *Skyfall* title sequence is one of the most beautiful ever to grace a cinema screen, and having Adele singing the title song is a definite bonus. I've watched the sequence many times on YouTube and it starts with Bond (Daniel Craig) plunging into a river, shot, presumed dead, and then plummeting slowly downwards to a blue marine world, encountering guiding hands, whirlpools, mirrors, Chinese dragons, skulls, graveyards, and countless other objects. The final image, a close-up of Daniel Craig's eye where the director's name, Sam Mendes, appears, is, I think, a nod to Saul Bass at the end of *Vertigo's* title sequence.

You can also, if you wish, listen to the Russian Army Choir reprising Adele's *Skyfall* song on YouTube. So, there is something the Russians envy about our culture then?

BOOKS

In this section I've collated the book reviews I've written for *Javelin*, *Tabloid*, and *Respect* and they are not arranged in any date order. The original reviews included the price but I've only included the title, author, and publisher here which should be sufficient if any reader wishes to track the book to buy or order from a library. Please bear in mind that some of these books may now be out of print, have a different publisher, or have a revised addition. It is recommended you only seek out the most recent edition for any book offering travel and health advice. They are divided into fiction and non-fiction categories.

Non-fiction

World Wise: Your Passport to Safer Travel
Mark Hodson and The Suzy Lamplugh Trust; Thomas Cook

Crammed within the 336 pages of this book is a wealth of information on travelling safely in virtually any country of the world. There are scores of essential tips on what to pack, travelling solo, taxi drivers, tricks that thieves will use to deprive you of your cash, culture shock on arrival and return, etc. There is also a handy directory of over 200 countries from Afghanistan to Zimbabwe where you can find out the country's religion(s), whether the tap water is drinkable, where the British embassy is, what vaccinations you need, and a host of other essential (and sometimes alarming!) information. Even if you don't intend to travel at all, the book still makes fascinating reading. Thoroughly recommended.

The Diving Bell and the Butterfly
Jean-Dominique Bauby; Fourth Estate

Bauby was the editor-in-chief of French *Elle* magazine and in 1995 he had a massive stroke which left him completely paralysed. By means of fluttering one eyelid he dictated this astonishing book which offers us an insight into his locked-in world and his views of the 'outside'. It is both desperately sad and strangely uplifting at the same time. A tribute to the human spirit and one which will make readers count their blessings. Bauby died in 1997, aged 45.

*[The book was filmed in 2007 with a screenplay by the playwright Ronald (*The Dresser*) Harwood. The film is in French with English subtitles.]*

What Falls Away
Mia Farrow; Bantam Books

Most film star memoirs tend to be marbled with fairly generous strands of gossip and acerbic character demolitions of colleagues and friends. However, Mia Farrow's account of her childhood, her two marriages to Frank Sinatra and André Previn, and her troubled relationship with Woody Allen, is told in rather an understated, unaffected, and dignified manner which does her credit. In an appendix she has reproduced the Supreme Court's decision in its entirety concerning her legal battle for custody of her children after Allen was found having an affair with one of her adopted daughters, Soon-Yi. The reader is left with the distinct impression that she was correct in bringing the case against Allen, as was the court's decision to grant her custody of the children.

Notes from a Small Island
Bill Bryson; Black Swan

It isn't often that I drop a book to the floor because it has rendered me weak with laughter. I did this several times with American Bill Bryson's bestseller *Notes from a Small Island*. He gives us his candid and witty views of the UK, its customs, and its people. Some examples: after partaking of a particularly hot curry in Bradford he talks of his fillings sizzling and his '... *stomach bubbling away like a heated beaker in a mad scientist movie'*. In London he was much taken with exotic station names like Stamford Brook, Maida Vale, and

Bromley-by-Bow. *'That isn't a city up there—it's a Jane Austen novel.'*

Neither Here nor There
Bill Bryson; Minerva

Here, Bryson casts his witty eye over Europe from Oslo to Istanbul. Just one example from his chapter on Rome: *'Romans park their cars the way I would park if I had just spilled a beaker of hydrochloric acid in my lap.'* Since its publication in 1991 this book has been reprinted an incredible twenty-eight times; four times this year alone. [*This review was written in 1996.*] With a bleak and dismal winter ahead, I commend both these books to you as literary antidepressants. They should save you raiding your winter stores of Prozac!

The Birds
Camille Paglia; BFI

Alfred Hitchcock's film *The Birds,* based on a Daphne du Maurier short story, remains one of my favourites from the master. Not just because of its technical wizardry for the time (1963) but because of the beautiful, almost surreal, depictions of the potential violence of nature, the cause never actually being explained in the film or story. Professor Camille Paglia has certainly gone to town on the film in her analysis of the film's mythical, technical, and aesthetic power. Some of her observations are very astute—she even comments on the film's title sequence where the titles are gradually chipped away as if by bird pecks. However, I think she sometimes overanalyses—for example, on the quotation marks Hitch insisted on around female lead Ms Hedren's childhood nickname, her forename 'Tippi'. They are said to resemble diving birds and become 'forceps' through which the director brought his star (a former model) to birth! Nevertheless, there is a wealth of technical information, a bibliography, and makes fascinating reading.

The Westmores of Hollywood
Frank Westmore and Muriel Davidson; W. H. Allen

The story of the genius family of George Westmore and his six sons, each of whom eventually became head of a Hollywood studio's make-up department. Fabulously powerful and successful, they paid a stiff price for their success in jealousy, betrayal, alcoholism, and suicide.

How Barbara Stanwyck was aged to over 100, how Frederic March was converted to Dr Jekyll and Shirley MacLaine into a geisha girl, are just some of the many effects described (with illustrations), but as well as being make-up geniuses, the Westmores were father confessors to the stars and many fascinating glimpses of the Hollywood legends past and present are presented. What remains though, is the tragedy of the Westmores; despite being the most respected technicians in their profession, they never seemed to get on with each other. Their story alone would make a riveting film.

Marie Curie
Robert Reid; Paladin

A detailed, sympathetic biography of a dedicated scientist and a remarkably stubborn and independent woman. This book follows the success of the BBC Two series *Marie Curie* (played by Jane Lapotaire), and although this edition was brought out in 1978, it was originally published in 1946. Fascinating reading, even for non-scientists.

Mr Harty's Grand Tour
Russell Harty; Century

Although Russell Harty was not my favourite TV personality, I found him an interesting mixture of snob and pleb. His book, *Mr Harty's Grand Tour*, may not tell you very much about the European countries he visited for his TV series, but it does offer fascinating glimpses of various characters, including his own. It is a gossipy book and although Harty's quixotic quest is undertaken in full 1980s comforts it is eminently readable. Here are his views on Paris pavement cafes:

80

'All the guide books of Paris say that one of its chief assets is its ... cafes where you sit for a lingering drink and examine the world as it passes ... I am much more aware of the passers by examining me [as if I'm in] ... a sort of fish tank. There is an interesting way of coping with this situation ... you [pretend] that you have to spend the night with the seventh person who walks ... past from left to right. There's something in this farrago to suit everybody, except the poor unwitting devil who happens to be the seventh [walking] past ...'

Although Harty was a broadcaster, journalist, and interviewer, this —as far as I know—is the only book he's published but he did adapt Iris Murdoch's story *Black Madonna* for TV. The book is no masterpiece but an interesting document from someone who was, incredibly, a Professor of English at the University of New York!

[Russell Harty died in June 1988 aged fifty-three, from liver failure caused by hepatitis B.]

Views from Abroad: The Spectator Book of Travel Writing
Philip Marsden-Smedley and Jeffrey Klinke (eds.); Grafton

If you seek a diverse collection of travel writing from 1950 to the present, you can do no better than *Views from Abroad*; its 466 pages are divided into eight sections: Travel and Travellers, Western Europe, Eastern Europe, Africa, The Middle East, Far East, Australia, Central and South America. The emphasis throughout is on the personal experience of 'being abroad' rather than foreign reporting.

Kingsley Amis asks if the travel book is dead, Freya Stark discusses the philosophy of travel, John Mortimer takes you round Reagan's America, and Ian Fleming discusses the pros and cons of living in the Caribbean. James Morris (who later became Jan Morris) contributes four articles—two as a male and two as a female. As James, he discusses the fading of borders and states there is little that is unfamiliar in modern travel—since TV has taken us there already— prescient since this was written in 1950! Later, he discusses a traumatic voyage from Egypt (where he worked as a journalist) back to England where he then studied at Oxford. As Jan Morris, she chastises the Venetian officials for not spending enough on the city's preservation yet confesses that time, tide, and preservationists have not destroyed it yet, in 1978 anyway. Whilst in Istanbul she stayed at the Perla Palace hotel and describes a phalanx of whirling swathed and turbanned girls suddenly erupting into a room hitherto listening to a waltz. They then disappear as quickly as they'd arrived. High jinks indeed in an article sombrely entitled 'Notes from a Dying City'.

This is a very small sample that the sixty-one contributors offer. My personal favourite was Alice Thomas Ellis's contribution on the phrase book which had the useful phrase: '*My friend whom you saw the other day died last night*'. As the blurb on the cover informs us, it really is a 'ticket to the purest form of travel and the deepest form of armchair'. Bon voyage.

Rich: The Life of Richard Burton
Melvyn Bragg; Hodder & Stoughton

Apart from being male, Welsh, and called Richard, I can claim no further similarities to the subject of Melvyn Bragg's biography, *Rich: The Life of Richard Burton*. Twenty-eight chapters and 533 pages attempt to cram fifty-nine years of life before us and Bragg, for the most part, marshals his material—anecdotes, interviews, Burton's notebooks—in a very readable format. The only section of the book which I thought a little folkloric was his early life in South Wales: drunken father, saintly mother, a dozen children squashed into a hovel, rugby, booze … Once the Hollywood era began and from the cataclysmic first meeting with Liz Taylor, the book takes on a sort of fluid urgency which grips until the end.

Burton emerges (mainly through his unpublished diary) as a literary scholar and indeed was asked if he wanted to become an Oxford don. His devotion to La Taylor is also apparent, having nursed her through countless illnesses and operations. Bragg's tone is never obtrusive and much of the book is told through other voices, especially Philip Burton's, the schoolmaster who gave our Welsh hero his stage name: he was born Richard William Jenkins. Although only a few of his fifty-five films deserve serious consideration (perhaps *Equus* and *Who's Afraid of Virginia Woolf?*) his merits as a human being are what this biography impresses on me.

It's Only a Movie, Ingrid
Alexander Walker; Headline

The title of Alexander Walker's memoir, *It's Only a Movie, Ingrid*, derives from a rebuff Hitchcock once made to Ingrid Bergman. Walker writes a weekly column for *The Evening Standard* and is the author of numerous books on cinema and its stars. In this delightful but un-sycophantic book, he recounts anecdotes of meetings with the like of Charlie Chaplin, Katherine Hepburn, Cary Grant, and Faye Dunaway, to name but a few.

The trials and tribulations of serving on the Cannes Film Festival jury, his physical assault on live television by Ken Russell, and his grilling by William Hearst to name his six best films of all time are some of the other highlights. Walker's honesty and integrity impress throughout and despite his doubt as to whether he's successfully analysing a film's merits or demerits, he is adamant of the 'pleasure it's been to bear witness'.

[Alexander Walker died in 2003, aged seventy-three.]

Bette and Joan: The Divine Feud
Shaun Considine; Sphere

It took Shaun Considine ten years to gather the material for his book on the two queen bees of Hollywood, Joan Crawford and Bette Davis. What started as a magazine article snowballed into a book when he discovered the extent of the venomous rivalry between the two stars. Surprisingly, they only appeared in one film together, the 1962 classic, *Whatever Happened to Baby Jane?*. It is the gossipy tales of their pranks behind (and during) the scenes that mark the book's most fascinating section. They actually started another film, *Hush Hush, Sweet Charlotte*, but Olivia de Havilland replaced Crawford when the bickering got out of hand. The early part of the book is a sort of alternating mini-biography and though diverting, is less fascinating than the duels on *Baby Jane* and *Charlotte*.

The book is not without humour. Crawford's secretary once rang Barbara Stanwyck, asking her to dine with the star at 5 p.m. When asked why on earth she wanted to dine so early, back came the reply that *'Miss Crawford's stomach was now on Eastern Standard Time since she'd just returned from holiday'*. Stanwyck retorted, *'Well, you can tell Miss Crawford that Barbara Stanwyck's stomach is on California time and has been for the last thirty years!'* Shakespeare it isn't, but for a lazy read, it's well worth a fiver.

[Joan Crawford died in 1972 and Bette Davis died in 1989. An excellent eight-part TV series entitled Feud, *about the two stars, aired in 2017 starring Jessica Lange as Joan Crawford and Susan Sarandon as Bette Davis.]*

Listening to Prozac; A Psychiatrist Explores Antidepressant Drugs and the Remaking of the Self
Peter Kramer; Fourth Estate

[This review was written for the Journal of Pharmaceutical Medicine *in 1994. The review has been amended to correct spelling mistakes in the original and explain some technical terms for the reader. These are in square brackets. The journal has now been discontinued. Prozac, a trade name for the drug fluoxetine, was launched by Eli Lilly in 1989.]*

Prozac (fluoxetine), like the benzodiazepines, *[the group of drugs comprising Valium, Librium, Mogadon, etc.]* has become something of a mass cultural phenomenon. It is the world's biggest selling antidepressant with annual sales of some $1.25 billion. The trade name Prozac will no doubt soon be in our dictionaries, spelt with a lower case 'p', affording it the ultimate honour of acceptance like hoover, biro, and aspirin, registered trademarks transmuted by wide usage into common nouns. Kramer's book has also become a bestseller, especially in the USA, where some four million people (not necessarily patients) are daily swallowing this green and white capsule. Elsewhere, another four million or so in nearly seventy countries are sending fluoxetine towards their troubled limbic systems *[the parts of the brain dealing with emotions, memory, and arousal]*.

Kramer's book comprises a series of detailed case studies, describing how Prozac dramatically altered the lives of his patients. Although other antidepressants lifted his patients' gloom, Prozac not only made them feel better but made them feel different. It made them feel more like they wanted to feel. On stopping the drug, many said, 'I am not myself any more.' But who had these patients been when they were not on medication? Had Prozac somehow removed a false self and replaced it with a true self? It is to this almost moral dilemma that Kramer devotes most of his book. In between these fascinating ruminations and case histories we are treated to a detailed history of the development of antidepressants and the story of how Prozac had been created. Kramer has now announced the arrival of the cosmetic psychopharmacological makeover.

The 'clean' nature of fluoxetine as opposed to the 'dirty' profile of the older agents is emphasised, and yet this specificity seems to lend itself to potentially very wide application in treating *formes frustes [amorphous disorders]*. Indeed two chapters are devoted to these; one on low self-esteem and one on inhibition of pleasure and sluggishness of thought. One tends to think we have arrived at Huxley's 'soma' in *Brave New World* but Kramer posits Walter Percy's last novel, *The Thanatos Syndrome*, as a better analogy. In the novel, an insidious chemical called Heavy Sodium is introduced into the water supply. By reducing human self-consciousness, the drug robs individuals of their souls, finally causing them to take on the postures and behaviours of apes. Whilst Kramer obviously never contemplates such an outcome with Prozac, he shares the moral ethicist's concern about 'mood brighteners' in general. He concludes by saying that in time '... we will come to discover that modern psychopharmacology has become, like Freud in his day, a whole climate of opinion under which we conduct our different lives'.

Kramer writes well and convincingly, although some sections are a little longer than they need be. I would question whether only Prozac would have benefited all his patients, since in one case, he reports equally dramatic results with sertraline, a drug with a similar mode of action. Perhaps I should mention that this review was written under the influence of about 200 ml of caffeinated coffee. I suspect this will be the nearest that most of us will come to a daily psychopharmacological makeover.

FICTION

Esau
Philip Kerr; Chatto & Windus

Starting off with a quote from Genesis, 'Behold Esau my brother is a hairy man and I am a smooth man', *Esau* introduces us to mountaineer Jack Furness, back from an expedition to the Himalayas with a skull he believes to be a fossil. Then we're introduced to Stella Swift, his girlfriend and a leading palaeontologist at the University of Berkeley. After much technical investigations by her, she is convinced that (a) the skull is not a fossil and (b) it is very recent and could conceivably point to the existence of the so-called Missing Link between chimps and man. They both plan an expedition back to the Himalayas and like all good adventure yarns, it seems one member of the expedition has motives other than what they may seem.

To complicate matters further, both India and Pakistan are on the verge of nuclear war and Time Is Not On Their Side! *Esau* is always gripping and although the ending has shades of Hilton's *Lost Horizon* about it, it is definitely a page turner. The film rights have been sold to Disney.

[Sadly, it seems the film never materialised!]

The Keys to the Street
Ruth Rendell; Hutchinson

Ruth Rendell is surely one of our most talented crime novelists and her latest novel *The Keys to the Street* will do her reputation no harm at all. Mary Jago has donated her bone marrow to a man she does not know. This act leads to her finishing with her boyfriend Alistair and sets up a train of mysterious, disturbing, and tragic events which involve a varied cross-section of people from the Regents Park area of London. Another page-turner from the co-Queen of crime; the other is P. D. James.

Audrey Hepburn's Neck
Alan Brown; Spectre

This first novel written by a BBC journalist is a touching evocation of the clash of American and Japanese cultures. Written in simple but effective prose it tells the story of Toshi, a twenty-three-year-old comic book artist who falls in love with his English teacher. Counterpoised against his dramatic and romantic encounters is his search for the reason his parents have split up and a revelation about his true nationality.

For once, the blurb on the cover is accurate; Brown makes '... cultural strangeness erotic'; 'perceptive and poignant'; '... a beautifully written novel'. Yes, I know the title is bizarre but I'll let you discover its meaning, in keeping with the mysterious Oriental style of the novel!

The Silver Castle
Clive James; Picador

Mention Clive James and the phrases that come to mind are cynical and witty. Those adjectives are best suited to his TV persona. As a novelist, with *The Silver Castle*, you can add sensitive, emotional, heart-warming, and affecting. This is the story of Sanjay who grew up in Bombay's slums. Obsessed with the magic and charm of Bollywood and its stars, he eventually gets a job as a film extra. However, interwoven with his rise to brief stardom, the story also follows his attempts to eke out a living in his meagre rented room and the friends and foreigners he meets during his quest. I won't give away the ending but the last few pages of this novel are amongst the most moving I've read for a long time. It is here that James diverts slightly from Sanjay's specific story and attempts a more universal summary of the plight of the many Sanjays of Bombay's streets. A novel which worries its way back into your mind but makes you glad that you've read it.

Fatal Cure
Robin Cook; Pan

The latest from Robin (*Coma*) Cook, master of the medical thriller. It concerns the plight of Drs Angela and David Wilson who give up practising medicine in the city to work in the rural Bartlett Medical Center. Here they hope to give their daughter, who has cystic fibrosis, a better quality of life and enjoy a less stressful lifestyle themselves. However, things soon start going wrong when patients with relatively good prognoses start dying without good cause. Like *Coma*, the game is guessing how and why. It will certainly keep you turning the pages and whilst the ending does seem a little rushed and somewhat implausible, Cook manages a very hefty swipe at the way private medicine is going, emphasising the financial rather than the medical constraints now facing doctors daily.

Gridiron
Philip Kerr; Vintage

I devoured *Gridiron*'s 370 pages in one day. The Gridiron is the world's most intelligent building, a 'smart' skyscraper whose every facet is controlled by a new breed of super computer called Ishmael. Strongly reminiscent of the HAL computer in *2001: A Space Odyssey*, it controls the lighting, heating, information systems, and ultimately, the fate of the people in the Gridiron. I cannot give any more of the plot away except to say that the action really starts when Ishmael's circuits accidentally get crossed with a child's computer game. The film rights have been sold already.

[Sadly, the film was never made!]

Good Grief
Keith Waterhouse; Sceptre

June Pepper, recently widowed, promised her husband Sam to keep a daily diary after his death. He believed this would enable her to come to terms with her loss. She doesn't keep her promise but instead talks to Sam (and the reader) with a 'stream of consciousness' about her thoughts about everything—from mundane daily tasks to her new male acquaintance whom she discovers has bought her husband's suit at Oxfam. Funny and sad in turns, this is a realistic and poignant tale of coming to terms with bereavement.

The Miracle Strain
Michael Cordy; Bantam Press

A first novel by someone who worked in marketing for ten years. His style is very Michael Crichton-ish, which, for most readers, will be a plus. The story concerns Tom Carter, a leading geneticist and doctor who has invented a revolutionary machine, the Genescope. This decodes a person's genes from one body cell and predicts the onset and nature of any disease they may be prone to, in addition to constructing a hologram representing the person. He discovers that his daughter has an incurable brain tumour and has only a year to live. In a frantic search for some form of gene therapy to save her, a secret brotherhood, 2,000 years old, come to his attention. They offer Carter the chance to decode the DNA of the most famous healer in history, Jesus Christ.

An extremely fast-paced thriller, which stretches one's credibility to the limit. However, it fulfils my basic requirement of Getting The Reader To Turn The Page. The film rights have been sold to Disney for $1.5 million.

[Sadly, yet again, the film was never made.]

The God of Small Things
Arundhati Roy; Flamingo

Winner of last year's Booker prize, *The God of Small Things* has much to commend it. The descriptions of baking hot Indian landscapes, the sweltering, stupefying heat, and a tragically fated illicit love affair are beautifully rendered here. There may sometimes be too much description and extraneous detail but one is soon drawn into the book's hypnotic spell. If you can imagine L. P. Hartley's *The Go-Between* transplanted to India, that is the nearest I can come to describing the flavour of the book.

[Arundhati Roy has refused permission for the book to be filmed.]

Bridget Jones's Diary
Helen Fielding; Picador

A hilarious read from start to finish, based on Fielding's column in the *Daily Mail*. Each day begins with secretary Bridget Jones's weight, number of cigarettes consumed, and often the number of 1471 calls she's made to check if her boyfriend rang. A joy to read since, beyond the humour, it has a ring of truth about it too.

253
Geoff Ryman; Flamingo

This novel was first published on the internet and is described as an Easi-Access novel. You can read it page by page if you wish, or just dip in and out of each page in any order. The author has taken as his setting a tube train on the London Underground, which, with driver included, has 253 passengers. Each page describes what each person's outward appearance is, some inside information on them, and what they are thinking and doing. Each page contains exactly 253 words. Some passengers are in a relationship with other passengers; others are travelling solo. It's a fascinating concept. It would have been even better if it was based on real people.

Picnic at Hanging Rock
Joan Lindsay; Penguin

On St Valentine's Day, 1900, a party of schoolgirls went on a picnic to Hanging Rock, near Macedon, Australia. Some were never to return. This chilling tale, framed as though it was a true story, was, in fact, entirely fictional. It is expertly written, both in terms of maintenance of tension and in the descriptions of the outstandingly beautiful Australian countryside. Why did the girls' watches all stop at midday, what was the red cloud that Edith Harton saw in the distance, and why did Miss McGraw, the governess, apparently roam about without her skirt?

This is not a book for people who like their mysteries neatly solved, but is, nevertheless, extremely readable for all that. It is written in such a way that ideas and images worry their way back into the mind, long after you've finished the book. *Picnic at Hanging Rock* has now been filmed starring Rachel Roberts and Dominic Guard, and directed by Peter Weir.

[In addition to Peter Weir's 1975 film, a six-part TV series was aired in 2018, starring Natalie Dormer as Miss Hester Appleyard, the headmistress. Directed by Michael Rymer, Larysa Kondracki and Amanda Brotchie, it was nominated for ten awards but did not win any. Peter Weir's film won two BAFTAs, one for Cinematography and one for Costume Design.]

Rebuilding Coventry
Sue Townsend; Methuen

In Sue Townsend's *Rebuilding Coventry*, the book's title alludes to Coventry Dakin, a housewife of extraordinary beauty who is married to bald and boring Derek, whose hobby is breeding tortoises. Coventry leaves him after accidentally killing their neighbour with an Action Man doll. She goes on the run to London, sleeps rough in cardboard boxes, cleans for an eccentric family of academics, and eventually finds her salvation with a Sloaney dosser called Dodo.

The book is brief (152 pages), terse, and perceptive and its short attention span style is a constant plus. Here is an example of Coventry's musings on her past and present circumstances: *'I'm a great believer in lists. Yesterday's list was: Order smokeless fuel; clean chimney; shave legs; pluck eyebrows; has Bella got my big whisk? Today's list is: Give myself up to the police? Try to live in London?'*

It is a book full of droll, energetic humour and although rather more laconic than her Adrian Mole books, it is no less entertaining for that.

TRAVEL

I wrote my first travel article in 1989, after visiting Turkey. I felt it complimented the photos I'd taken and enabled me to share my experiences with people who hadn't been there or allowed comparisons with those who had. I enjoyed writing them, and on a re-reading, I noticed that all of them contain references to films. It seems that the compartments in my brain dealing with travel and films are very porous! The Portugal, St Lucia, and Prague articles were written for *Respect* magazine and the remainder for the *Tabloid* newspaper.

New York

> *'You have to be a little crazy to live in New York ...*
> *Crazy about shows, restaurants, theatres, shopping ...'*

New York subway poster

It is said that when one speaks of America, one really means New York and for New York, one really means Manhattan. Most visitors to New York do stay in Manhattan but it does have four other boroughs—Brooklyn, Queens, the Bronx, and Staten Island.

I did not expect to be enthusiastic about New York. A multitude of crime series, films, and news reports had prepared me for the worst. You will be assaulted, but by sensory overload—visually and aurally rather than physically. The skyscrapers, glass and concrete leviathans which crowd out the sky itself, will be your first 'assassins'.

Some are incredibly beautiful, their mirrored windows reflecting a myriad other scrapers that will drain your camera of film at an incredible rate.

There is, for instance, the silvery Chrysler building, built in the 1930s, its long spire causing it to appear like an enormous hypodermic, ready to puncture the belly of a passing helicopter, plane, or cloud. Helicopters are a frequent sight, busy black locusts monitoring the skyline and depositing billionaire executives on their private helipads.

There is too the elegant Empire State Building, built in 1931, its eighty-sixth-floor observatory affording a magnificent panorama of the city and shoreline by day or night. At its base you will find a Guinness World of Records exhibition.

The Empire State Building is not now the tallest building in the world (that's the Sears Tower, Chicago), nor is it the tallest in New York; that's the World Trade Center, where you can zoom 107-storeys high in fifty-eight seconds. Look out too for the octagonal Pan-Am building and the red Noguchi Cube near the Marine Midland Bank (140 Broadway): its tiptoeing pose looks decidedly precarious. It was designed by Isamu Noguchi in 1968.

Need a break from the concrete jungle? Head for Central Park, but only in daytime. It's both illegal and dangerous to enter the park at night. It's two and a half miles long and half a mile wide. It took twenty years to complete and since 1876 has been New Yorkers' pride and joy for picnics, sports, theatre, concerts, and just plain walking. When I was there, the Mayor of New York, David Jenkins, turned up in shorts and cap to play tennis after making a speech about how New Yorkers should support their park. There followed an embarrassing song sung by him and the park committee called *You Gotta Have Park*. This motto was available on caps and T-shirts on sale afterwards.

On 72nd Street, Central Park West, you'll see the Dakota building, where poor Mia Farrow was 'bedevilled' in Polanski's *Rosemary's Baby*; the building was renamed *The Bramford* in the film. I've always thought it had an evil chill that matched any satanist. Now it's home to Lauren Bacall, Leonard Bernstein, and Yoko Ono. It was here that John Lennon was murdered by a psychotic 'fan' and my earlier bad vibes about the Dakota seem more justified than ever.

Shopping, whether window or otherwise, is a delight in New York. All the famous names are here: Tiffany's, Saks, Bloomingdales, and Macy's, the world's biggest department store. You will be continually persuaded by attractive staff to try a new perfume, aftershave, cosmetic, or, as I was, a new toothpaste at only twelve dollars a tube! For toys, then FAO Schwarz is the store for you, where you can buy a doll's house for a mere 10,000 dollars. The Trump Tower is worth a visit, if only for the marvellous gold décor, reminiscent of a *Goldfinger* set, and internal mini-waterfalls.

A tour of the shoreline by boat is a must to survey Manhattan and the other boroughs. The best one goes from Pier 83 at the West End of 42nd Street. A three-hour trip (with commentary) is only fifteen dollars. You can even see the Bronx, where most of Tom Wolfe's *Bonfire of the Vanities* was set, and location filming of his novel has caused yet more racial tension in this troubled borough. For a more uplifting end to your day, why not visit the United Nations (East 42nd Street)? It's unusual in that it's actually on international rather than USA territory and its Security Council is most impressive, rather reminiscent of the War Room in Kubrick's *Dr. Strangelove*. Guided tours are available for about five dollars and leave every twenty minutes. The Statue of Liberty is, for many, the symbol of New York, although it was actually built by two Frenchmen, Bartholdi and Eiffel (of that Paris tower fame). Catch a ferry from Battery Park (Lower Manhattan) and take a lift up to the crown. Alternatively you can fly over the statue by helicopter—fifteen minutes costs about forty-five dollars.

New York has been described both as the most exciting city in the world and as the Calcutta of the Western Hemisphere. Which is correct? Neither and yet both. There is an incredible contrast between the wealthy and poor areas and yet it is these contradictory faces which contribute to its fascination. I'm sure that once you've tasted the Big Apple, you'll soon return for another bite.

Ten things you should know about New York and the USA.

[My trip was undertaken in May 1990, so many things have changed now, namely the sad, wilful destruction of the World Trade Center in 2001. The world's tallest building (in 2018) is now the Burj Khalifa in Dubai. Visa requirements, sales taxes, and a host of other things will no doubt have changed also but one possible change for the better is that the murder rate in New York currently appears to be less than that of London. The list below is what I wrote in 1990.]

1. Currency is US dollars. Some garages will not accept cash late at night and, without a credit card, you could be stuck. All the notes from one to 100 dollars look very similar.

2. Tipping is a way of life in America. In a restaurant, a tip of around 10–15% will be expected, unless the service was poor, which it rarely is. A sales tax of around 8% will be added to just about everything you buy.

3. Food on the whole is incredibly good, both in quality and quantity. Ask for a small Coke and you virtually get a bucketful, usually with half a pound of ice added. Requesting a salad delivers a rainforest to your plate.

4. There are many ways to travel round New York, but the quickest and cheapest is by foot. Pedestrians often move faster than the traffic. Otherwise, take a cab, but it must be a yellow cab; other taxis will inevitably rip you off. The subway is cheap, but the maps are complicated and it's dirty and noisy. Avoid the subway at night, especially if you're alone.

5. Although New York has a high crime rate (about four murders a day and some 200 muggings) common sense should ensure your safety. Wear a money-belt, stick to brightly lit main streets at night, and try not to behave like a tourist (poring over maps and looking up at skyscrapers).

6. Manhattan is for the most part laid out on a grid system. The central spine is Fifth Avenue. All areas to the west of it are known as West Side, while the East Side covers the area between Fifth Avenue and the East River. Avenues run north-south and streets run east-west.

7. Despite the fact that we share the same language with Americans, you may be confused by certain words or phrases. A private toilet is a 'bathroom', whilst a public one is a 'restroom'. A 'check' is a bill and a 'billfold' is a wallet; a 'pocketbook' is a handbag. 'Gas' (or gasoline) is petrol.

8. New York is five hours behind GMT. Americans use the twelve-hour clock for timetables. Make sure that if your bus leaves at 8 o'clock whether that means 8 a.m. or 8 p.m. Dates are written in month/day/year order.

9. Currently for entry to the USA, you do not need a visa but you will need a visa waiver form declaring you are not a criminal, a communist, or drug abuser. (In 1981 when Quentin Crisp wanted to emigrate to the US, he was asked at the American Embassy in London

if he was a practising homosexual; he replied that he didn't need to practice and that he was already perfect.)

10. Apart from making sure your tetanus and polio boosters are up to date, no special immunisations are required for the USA. Health care is incredibly expensive so make sure you have adequate travel insurance.

Further Reading
New York (Berlitz). Excellent pocket guide with useful maps.
The Rough Guide to New York by Martin Dunford and Jack Holland (Harrap-Columbus). Useful for more detailed background and fascinating insights into culture and contexts. I'd have found this fascinating even if I wasn't going to New York!

NEW ORLEANS

In Tennessee Williams' play *A Streetcar Named Desire*, set in New Orleans, the heroine mutters dreamily that she '… has always been dependent on the kindness of strangers'. Well, in New Orleans (or N'awlins), you may not be dependent on the kindness of strangers, but you will certainly experience it. This famed Southern hospitality is, I think, a kind of exuberance which can range from a 'Go for it,' from a hotel clerk changing your traveller's cheques, to a cheery 'How y'all doing?' from a waitress. Yes, they may say it to everyone, but it feels as if they're just saying it to you.

New Orleans is the largest port in the USA and the second largest in the world, after Amsterdam. Its population is about half a million but nearly twice that come to the city in conventions alone each year. N'awlins can boast some superlatives. For instance, the Greater New Orleans Causeway, a twenty-three-mile-long bridge spanning Lake Pontchartrain, is the largest in the world. Attention all football fans, for now we come to another world record, the Superdome. Lying like an enormous discoid spaceship in downtown New Orleans, this is the largest covered stadium in the world. Four years in the making and finished in 1975, it can comfortably seat 77,000 for a football game and 87,500 for a concert. The air conditioning unit alone weighs 9,000 tons. Guided tours are available and if you like absorbing masses of facts, you'll love it.

No visit to N'awlins would be complete without a trip down the Mississippi and what better way to see it than from a steamboat. One of the most famous is the *Natchez*, or there are more modest ones such as the *Voyageur* which will take you on a five-hour trip for about nine dollars. You can stop off at the historic Chalmette Battlefield, where the British were defeated at the Battle of New Orleans in 1815. Further down the river you enter swamp and bayou country and you may see some of the many alligators roaming these parts. (I only saw one dead gator floating face down.) Unless you're very interested in seeing the steel and concrete structures of New Orleans' oil industry, you may find a large portion of the trip rather monotonous and non-photogenic!

What about all that jazz? Head for Jackson Square at the heart of the French Quarter. In the morning, call in for breakfast, as most of N'awlins seems to, at the Café du Monde. There are only five items on the menu. Fresh orange juice, coffee, milk, hot chocolate, and beignets. These are square, doughnut-like confections, covered in icing sugar, and are absolutely delicious. Whilst you eat this scrumptious and calorific fare, you will be serenaded by jazz musicians nearby and they even play requests.

At night there is no shortage of jazz clubs such as Preservation Hall (St. Peter Street) or Pat O'Brien's, famous for its 29-oz. Hurricane lamp style glasses. A Hurricane is a blend of rum and passionfruit juice; you'll have to pay a deposit of two dollars for the glass, since many take them home as souvenirs!

Apart from the jazz, there are slightly more dubious places of the night to entice you, but with so many people on the streets, it is generally safe to walk around the French Quarter in the evening.

If you'd prefer a quieter end to your day, try Top of the Mart (2, Canal Street), the world's largest cocktail lounge. What about sampling Miss New Orleans? I hasten to add that this is a delicious cocktail of peach juice, cream, crushed ice, and schnapps. As you survey the city beneath you, well you are thirty-three-storeys high, you may experience a floaty buzz and the feeling that New Orleans is spinning around you. Don't worry, it's the cocktail lounge that's revolving, once every ninety minutes or three feet a minute. Don't leave your belongings on the windowsill. That doesn't revolve, and you'll soon be parted from them. The vista of that burnished coppery-gold snake below, the Mississippi at sunset, is one which will be forever etched in my memory.

When you're done with the French Quarter and the Mississippi, then the Garden District deserves your attention. Take a streetcar; the one named *Desire* alas no longer runs, but plenty of others do and it's only sixty cents wherever your destination. The Garden District is a vast residential area with beautifully large balconied houses, colonial style, and a marked contrast to the more cramped ones in the French Quarter. On your way back, visit the Confederate Museum (929, Camp Street), for a look at battle flags, weapons, and Robert E. Lee's personal effects from the Civil War. Books on military surgery and surgical instruments are also on display and make for fascinating, if gruesome, viewing.

There are some superb shopping malls in New Orleans. The Jax Brewery, opposite Jackson Square, has sixty shops where you can buy anything from toys to posters to clothes and food. For designer goods go to Canal Place (333, Canal Street) where you'll find Gucci, Laura Ashley, Guy La Roche, et al. My four days in New Orleans allowed me to see all that I've described; you may feel you want to stay longer, but be warned about those beignets. You could end up paying excess baggage on your return flight home—on yourself!

Four things you should know about New Orleans
[Trip undertaken in May 1990]

1. A sales tax of 9% will be added to all items that you buy.

2. New Orleans can get very hot and humid. In May (when I was there), the temperature was seldom below 85–90° Fahrenheit. Hotel rooms, cars, and shops are air-conditioned.

3. Food, as in New York, is good both in quality and quantity. You will see dishes referred to as Cajun or Creole. Cajun cooking originated with country folk living in rural Louisiana whilst Creole dishes were developed by French and Spanish city dwellers. Creole food will usually be hot and spicy, but not always.

4. New Orleans is six hours behind GMT.

[Sadly, in 2005, Hurricane Katrina did its worst and battered poor New Orleans, killing some 1,800 people and causing some $81 billion worth of damage. The Top of the Mart cocktail lounge is no more, but in my mind, I sometimes still gaze down at that golden Mississippi, a Miss New Orleans in my hand.]

Further Reading
New Orleans by Susan Poole (Frommer's). Excellent text, less good with maps.
USA (Berlitz). Covers all the USA and the small section on New Orleans covers the essentials.

Portugal

The stream of images that go through one's head in thinking of Portugal are probably connected (erroneously) to visions of a smaller version of Spain: port, sardines, and the inevitable but popular Algarve beaches and golf clubs. However, '*Algarve nao e Portugal*' (The Algarve is not Portugal) is a phrase used by the Portuguese and one to be heeded. A visit to Portugal's capital, Lisbon (or Lisboa), its western coast, and the Alentejo plains has much to commend it and formed the basis of my week there. Portugal was (incredibly) not a democracy until 1974, and many Portuguese still recall António Salazar's republic: the strict censorship of almost everything and the feared secret police. It is difficult to reconcile such recent events with Portugal's now booming economy and its busy preparations for Expo 98, which will celebrate an oceanic theme, based on the country's contribution to navigation and exploration from the likes of Da Gama and Magellan. Although currently huge cranes loom over the city, there is still much to savour, for example:

Along the twenty-mile waterfront by the River Tagus you will see the Ponte 25 de Abril suspension bridge, the longest in Europe and reminiscent of the one in San Francisco. At its other end is a smaller version of the Christ the King (Cristo Rei) statue in Rio de Janeiro. There is a small souvenir shop in the head!

Along the same waterfront there are two landmarks which have almost become icons for Lisbon. Firstly, The Torre de Belem, a famous decorative sixteenth century tower which gives the impression of a ship about to sail out to sea. Secondly, there is the Monument to the Discoveries, jutting out from the riverbank like a ship's prow cresting a wave. At its head is Prince Henry the Navigator, gazing out over the Tagus. Nearby is an impressive Coach Museum and the beautiful Jerónimos Monastery.

Briefly, other highlights (by no means exhaustive) are the Elevador de Santa Justa, an outside lift, originally powered by steam and built in 1902, not by Gustav Eiffel as rumour has it, but by Meisner. Another is the Gulbenkian Museum opened in 1955 by an Armenian billionaire who owned 5% of the Iraq Petroleum Company. The Lalique glass collection is particularly impressive and finally there is the Edward VII Park, a beautiful place to stretch your legs near the centre of the city and overlooked by the Miraparque Hotel, where I stayed.

Around Lisbon

If you seek a 'resort' type holiday then Estoril and Cascais, some fifteen miles from the capital, are for you. Estoril is very chic and cosmopolitan and even boasts a casino with some 200 croupiers. Cascais is slightly less glitzy but no less popular and fishermen and tourists mingle happily together. The highlight for me though was Sintra, some sixteen miles north-west of Lisbon. Byron never had a good word to say about Portugal but in a letter to his mother he described the village of Sintra as: '... *perhaps the most delightful in Europe ... It unites in itself all the wildness of the Western Highlands with the verdure of the South of France*'. Towering over Sintra, on a high hillside, is Pena Palace; a nineteenth century fantasy built for Queen Maria II. It is a curious amalgam of various architectural styles and its pink and yellow colours convey the bizarre impression of a giant Battenberg cake that has somehow gone curiously wrong!

Nearby you can cool off on a beach called Praia Grande where the wild Atlantic waves create a constant mist of sea spray and ozone, rendering the myriad tourists into hazy Lowry-like figures in the far distance. A nearby hotel will allow you to swim in their Olympic-size pool for a few pounds but the waves from the Atlantic even spill over into that—so be warned. Further up the beach is Cabo da Roca, the most westerly point in Europe. A lonely lighthouse marks the spot and a nearby shop will sell you a certificate to verify your geographic location. It is always windy here; my baseball cap is now winging its way towards the USA.

Some twenty miles north-west of Lisbon the coastal resort and fishing village of Ericeira has some excellent beaches for surfing. One thing the guidebooks won't tell you is that the grill-covered caves on the rocks used to house Salazar's prisoners prior to Portugal's democracy in 1974. (This information came from my Portuguese friend, Carlos.) Sobreira, some five miles inland from Ericeira, is a sort of mock village created by sculptor Jose France in the mid-sixties. It has windmills, watermills, a bakery, cobbler's shop, and several other attractions which make a worthwhile stop.

Berlenga Island

The tiny island of Berlenga (six miles off the western coast) is home to thousands of seabirds, a lighthouse, and a fortress with monastery. The crossing can only be made in the summer months from Peniche, a pleasant fishing village, but be warned, the journey can be rough. Black plastic bags are distributed at the start of your fifty-minute journey. Luckily mine was not full on my arrival; others were not so fortunate. On arrival, you'll probably think you've arrived on the set of Hitchcock's *The Birds*. Gulls and all manner of other seabirds crowd the rocks, swoop low overhead, and generally create a cacophony that takes some getting used to. A pleasant cove provides a small sandy beach, a cave to shelter in, and dark green crème de menthe water for swimming. Two cafes and a camping site are about the only other amenities on the island, but it still makes a worthwhile trip.

Évora and the Alentejo Plain

The Land Beyond the Tagus (*alem tejo* in Arabic) is a hot and dusty plain, scattered with olive and cork trees and occasional hillside fortresses, but its pièce de résistance is undoubtedly the walled city of Évora. The city is ninety-three miles east of Lisbon and in 1986 was declared a World Heritage site by UNESCO. The early settlement dates back to 59 BC. The key places of interest are the Roman Temple of Diana with its fourteen Corinthian columns, Sé Cathedral, and the fascinating, if gruesome, church of Sao Francisco with its Capela dos Ossos (Chapel of Bones). The bones of some 5,000 monks were used as architectural building blocks for this bizarre shrine but its most chilling feature is the sign above the entrance: *'Nós ossos que estamos aqui, aguardamos a chegada dos seus ossos'* or *'We bones that are here, await the coming of your bones'*. After that, refresh your senses with a visit to the charming town of Arraiolos, thirteen miles to the north of Évora, famed for its Moorish-Persian carpets. Expensive, but very beautiful. There's also a grand panorama over the plain from a ruined hilltop castle.

Finally, the people. It is always difficult to generalise about a whole race or nation, but one can only speak as one finds. I'll let Lord Carnarvon sum up my feelings about the Portuguese with this quote made in 1827: *'Portuguese politeness is delightful because it is by no means ... artificial, but flows in great measure from a natural kindness of feeling.'*

Five things you should know about Portugal

[Trip undertaken July 1997]

1. The currency is the escudo [it was in July 1997] which is rather confusingly represented by a dollar sign. [Since 2002, the currency is now the euro.]

2. Driving in Portugal can be a nightmare but standards are said to be improving. The road traffic accident rate is the second highest in the world (the first is North Korea). Some maintain Portugal is trying hard to gain first position. They drive on the right (usually). Some

103

country roads are very narrow and potholed. Be very careful if you intend to drive and take care as a pedestrian also!

3. The tap water is drinkable.

4. Portuguese is the seventh most widely spoken language in the world. A little knowledge of French, Spanish, or Italian may help you with translating signs but pronunciation is difficult. The language seems to have lots of soft 'sh' noises in it which gives the impression one is whispering or being confided in and treated to a succession of secrets.

5. Taxis are relatively cheap and Lisbon also has trams, buses, and a Metro system.

Further Reading
Lisbon (Berlitz)
Portugal (Berlitz)
The Lonely Planet Portugal Guide (Lonely Planet). A very detailed and comprehensive guide.
Essential Portugal (AA). A good alternative to the Berlitz guides
Introduction to Portugal (Julia Wilkinson; The Guide Book Company). Gives a more historical and cultural approach to the country.

The Caribbean
St Lucia and the Grenadines

'Underneath the mango tree me honey
And me come search for the moon
Underneath the mango tree me honey
And me make boolooloop soup* soon.'
[*Jamaican for making love]

Whilst singing these words, Miss Ursula Andress waded out of the Caribbean Sea as Honey Chile in 1962 in *Dr. No*. As a ten-year-old 'cinemagoer', I suppose this was my first introduction to the Caribbean although I somehow imagined that palm trees, sand like white talcum powder, and a sea vaguely reminiscent of pale lime juice was the product of an art director's efforts rather than something which existed in reality. Well, St Lucia will not disappoint, although Miss Andress will, most likely, not be on your beach.

St Lucia belongs to the Lesser Antilles Windward group and is midway between Martinique and St Vincent. The flight from London takes about nine to ten hours, depending on whether you stop off at Barbados to refuel on the way. St Lucia (pronounced locally as Loosha) boasts some impressive scenery, namely two peaks known as The Pitons, a drive-in volcano, and some very picturesque bays. The interior of the island is mainly rainforest and there seem to be banana plantations everywhere. The island is twenty-seven miles long and fourteen miles wide and home to about 140,000 people. The international airport is at Hewanorra in the south and is some ninety minutes' drive from the main resort areas to the north. The natives either speak English or a French patois which will probably defeat your comprehension even if you're quite fluent in French.

Since eating out can be dear in the Caribbean, many resort hotels are run on an all-inclusive basis where you can snack and drink to your heart (or stomach's) content. One such hotel is Club St Lucia on the Cap Estate, a 150,000-acre site on the north of the island. Accommodation is in single-storey bungalow blocks spread out over the grounds. Some can be quite a distance from the three restaurants, two pools, and activity centres but it does make it feel less like a hotel. It's also a popular place for weddings; three to five a day by my reckoning and hearing 'Here Comes the Bride' on bongo drums for what seems like the 100th time may be rather disconcerting. This may not be the best choice of holidays for singles!

Around the island and beyond

Be sure to break away from your closeted complex to see something of the island beyond. Soufrière is advertised as the world's only drive-in volcano and is well worth a visit. You'll soon get used to the sulphurous fumes and the multi-coloured rocks (green for copper, white for lime, and yellow for sulphur) should raise the eyebrows of the most jaded geologist. Efforts are being made to harness the steam energy for geothermal use but have been unsuccessful so far. One wonders if they need it because of the high monthly temperatures.

Nearby on the coast are the two cone-shaped Piton mountains— Gros Piton and Petit Piton rising majestically over the little town of Soufriere. Most people arrive here by boat and when leaving are treated to displays of local boys diving for coins (which the tourists are expected to throw at them from the boat)! Most trips involve a visit to Marigot Bay, one of the most beautiful and perfect yachting bays in the world. It was here that some of the scenes for *Doctor Dolittle* were filmed in 1966 and one almost expects Rex Harrison to creep round a palm tree and start singing to the animals. The island has been something of a movie star itself since scenes from *Firepower*, *Water*, and *Superman II* were also filmed here.

The capital, Castries, has rather a tired and jaded look to it and a visit to the local markets for food or clothes will take up half the day but there is little to detain you longer. There is a duty-free complex at Pointe Seraphine near the harbour but the prices do not seem to justify the 'duty-free' label.

A thirty-minute trip in a ten-seater plane will take you to the Grenadine group of 100 islands, only eight of which are inhabited. The group includes Bequia, a favourite with the likes of Princess Margaret and Fergie, and a true desert island feel prevails. One almost expects Sue Lawley to creep up on you and ask you to nominate your favourite records. Crystal clear water and pearlescent white sand make the Grenadines a snorkelling or a scuba paradise; an underwater camera should yield some beautiful shots of tropical fish.

To sum up, St Lucia can offer a lazy and relaxing environment if you want to swim, sunbathe, read, and do some water sports or a little island hopping. Bear in mind that the heat may curtail your enthusiasm for these and the night-time entertainment at your resort may be a little on the amateur side. However, there are many more Caribbean islands to explore; whichever one you choose will, I'm sure, provide similar pleasures to St Lucia or more.

Seven things you should know about St Lucia

[Trip undertaken June 1996]

1. The currency is the East Caribbean Dollar (EC$). You are advised to take cash or traveller's cheques in US$.
2. Throughout the year, the temperature will hover around the mid-80s Fahrenheit. The coolest and driest months are December/April. May/June and October/November are wet. Hurricanes are rare, but if they do occur they usually choose September to arrive.
3. The tap water is drinkable and there are no compulsory vaccinations although hepatitis A and typhoid are recommended. (If you're staying in a good quality hotel you're at relatively low risk.)
4. Never underestimate the strength of the Caribbean sun, even on cloudy days or whilst in the water. You'll soon realise why Factor 50+ sunscreen is on sale!
5. St Lucians drive on the left (usually)! The standard of driving leaves something to be desired and the state of the roads, even up to some high-class hotels, can be poor. The drive from the airport to the Cap Estate in the north has many hairpin bends and several people chose to do the return trip to the airport by helicopter; only US$35 and it only takes fifteen minutes.
6. On hotel and restaurant bills there is a government tax of 8% and a service charge of 10%. In some cases these are included in the price, so always check first. A departure tax of EC$27 is payable in cash at the airport.
7. Crime is not prevalent although it is obviously common sense not to display your wealth whilst walking down dark alleyways. Most hotels have a safe deposit box you can rent.

Further Reading
Southern Caribbean (Berlitz)
Caribbean Cruising by Emma Stanford (AA Publishing)

CZECHOSLOVAKIA
Prague
or Checking Out Your 'Prague-nosis'

In 1998 I went on a four-day trip to Prague and in order to give a concise summary of the trip, decided to write it in bite-size chunks in a Q&A format.

So where is Prague?

In the Czech Republic. Prague is its capital (since 1993). Prior to then, Prague was the capital of Czechoslovakia which is now split into the Czech Republic and Slovakia.

Is it easy to get to?

Very. Czech Airlines fly direct from Manchester in about two hours.

What's the currency?

The Czech crown (Kč).

A brief overview of Prague's layout please?

It is conveniently divided into four quarters:
The Castle District
The Lesser Town
The Old Town
The New Town
And the city is nicely bisected by the River Vltava on which you can take a leisurely cruise to get some superb views of the city.

Some highlights—things in the 'must see' category?

Prague Castle

Now home to Václav Havel, President of the Czech Republic, this impressive castle dominates the city. It houses St Vitus Cathedral, last resting place of St Wenceslas; the stained-glass windows are magnificent. The guards which protect the castle wear uniforms designed by the costume designer of *Amadeus*—and very smart they look too. The costume designer was Theodor Pištěk—and no, I'm not taking the, er, Michael!

Charles Bridge

Work started on this pedestrian aorta into the city in 1357 and some attribute its longevity to the fact that it's on a ley line, or even the thousands of medieval eggs in its mortar. It now has scores of hawkers, buskers, and artists flanking its sides and a stroll along the bridge, listening to scores of foreign accents, is like travelling along some cosmopolitan travelator tuning in and out of foreign frequencies. The bridge is a favourite haunt of pickpockets so be warned.

Vyšehrad

A suburb of Prague, this offers beautiful views of the city. At the Church of SS Peter and Paul you can visit the graves of notable Czech composers such as Antonín Dvořák.

What about the food?

Czech cuisine is often said to be all dumpling- and fat-based but I found the food to be of good quality and cheap. A three-course meal with a drink seldom cost more than £6. A bottle of beer costs about 80p. The beer in Prague is excellent and they have a huge variety.

And transport?

There is an excellent and cheap Metro system. A one-day ticket costs about £1.50. Taxis can be a rip-off and always agree the price first.

The language?

Most Czechs speak German or English but here are a few essential Czech phrases:

Hello: Dobry Den
Please: Prosim
Thank you: Dekuji
Yes: Ano
No: Ne

Oh yes—I believe you can easily get Semtex in Prague?

Yes. It's a soft drink, rather like Lucozade. Gives you explosive energy!

Would you go again?

Definitely!

Can you recommend any guidebooks?

Plenty. The following are all excellent. The Berlitz and AA guides are nice and compact to carry. The Time Out guide is the most critical and cynical and even alarmist about crime and crossing the road. This does require great care since traffic rarely stops at designated crossings.

Berlitz *Prague* Guide
AA *Essential Prague*
Time Out Guide *Prague*
AA City Pack *Prague*
Eyewitness Travel Guide *Prague*

Turkey

Mention Turkey to the uninitiated and images of *Midnight Express* will probably flood into their minds. It was a superb film, but hardly unbiased and not one to bring a smile to the face of the Turkish Tourist Board. The reality for the tourist (sorry, traveller) is, I'm pleased to say, immensely more optimistic. I have recently returned from my third trip to this fascinating country and I'm rapidly running out of superlatives for its attractions.

I visited Ölüdeniz (literally: Dead Sea) on the Mediterranean coast of Turkey; flights are to Dalaman, ninety minutes away from the resort by coach. Had Mother Nature been commanded to create a haven of outstanding natural beauty, then her answer would probably have been Ölüdeniz. Had Ansel Adams and David Hockney been employed as visual consultants, one would hardly be surprised: soaring mountain peaks dotted with pine trees slope down to a sparkling crème de menthe lagoon against an impossibly white spit of a shore. Everything seems designed to give the retina a continuous buzz, to invite gasps of admiration, temptations to dive in and to photograph it, although not necessarily in that order.

The resort is split into two main areas, Ölüdeniz and Olu Ata (or Hisaronu). Ölüdeniz comprises the lagoon and beach area and also hosts the higher-priced hotels. For instance, the Hotel Mei, which has its own beach on one side of the lagoon (admission: 5,000 Turkish lira or about £1.75). Accommodation is in little bungalows dotted over the steep hillside. An army of waiters constantly parade the beach, ready to take your orders for drinks and snacks. Olu Ata on the other hand is much less sophisticated up in the hills, about twenty minutes' drive

111

from Ölüdeniz. Here one finds small pensions, village rooms, and hotels fairly close together. It is kinder on the pocket and is some ten degrees cooler than its neighbour, no small consideration in peak season. Olu Ata is also a convenient base to visit the deserted 'ghost' village of Kaya.

Kaya was populated by the Greeks until the 1923 exchange of populations between Greece and Turkey which left the village deserted. It has two large churches, although the murals are sadly defaced. Even in broad daylight there is a slightly unsettling atmosphere present, but it's worth a visit. The focal point of this area, Fethiye, a very old town of about 20,000 population, was named after a Turkish pilot who crashed his plane there in the First World War. The town was devastated by an earthquake in 1958, leaving only a mosque and a school standing. Our courier told us they recur every thirty-one years but I think it's still there. There is an attractive harbour, a yacht marina, scores of cafes, and even a fairground and a Chinese restaurant. A busy market area and a good selection of shops for leather, honey (*bal*), and cotton goods make Fethiye worth a visit. There are no banks or pharmacies (*eczane*) in Ölüdeniz or Ata but Fethiye hosts plenty of these and a large bus station enabling you to explore the region further.

Amongst the trips you can take is one to the Dalyan river estuary. It was here that David Bellamy filmed the turtle breeding ground on the famous Turtle Beach. You can also cover yourself in black mud from the Dalyan river and wash it off in the nearby hot springs. It is reputed to rejuvenate, cure a hangover, and also be an aphrodisiac. It is rumoured that Elizabeth Arden uses such mud in her face packs, so ladies, if you want to take some home—good luck at Customs!

Thirty miles from Fethiye is the ruined city of Xanthos, once the capital of Lycia, where you can see the remains of a once fine amphitheatre and some impressive rock tombs. About ten miles further is the tiny village of Kalkan, which has a pleasant yacht marina and a good array of shops. I had lunch at the Pirate Hotel, where I tasted the best chicken I've ever had. Nearby is Patara, a resort whose only asset seems to be a sandy beach fifteen miles long; the sea was as warm as bathwater.

The highlight of this trip for me was Pamukkale (literally: Cotton Castle). However, it did involve a five-hour trip by dolmus, a type of minibus crammed with people. Dolmus means 'stuffed' in Turkish. It was well worth it; the sight that greeted me on arrival was an unlikely, beautiful, and strangely disconcerting landscape. From afar, it looks like a limestone quarry. On closer inspection, there are gleaming travertines, white and black stalactites supporting pools of shallow warm water. The surrounding landscape is one of arable fields and one gets the impression that an alien hand has simply dropped this white scar on the ground. Admission to the ridge is about 35p and it is on the clifftop where you will find the most expensive hotels (almost £25 for a single room). I can thoroughly recommend Pamukkale—take very dark glasses and plenty of film.

I stayed at the cliff base at the Konak Sade hotel. A single room with breakfast and dinner was £14. Lovely stripped pine furniture, hot and cold shower, flush toilet (a luxury in Turkey), a large swimming pool, and a super view of the ridge makes it an affordable and very pleasant stay. Across the road is the Pamukkale tourist office, where you can book your return trip. A single trip costs £2.50 back to Fethiye. This beautiful country is getting more popular every year and I hope that an over-commercialised Costa-type atmosphere does not swamp its current attractions. I fear this may already be happening in places like Bodrum on the Aegean coast. The trouble about waxing lyrical over a place is that yet more people will swamp it, although building is restricted in the Olu Ata region since it is almost the equivalent of our National Trust.

I have re-read my account so far and there is a glaring deficiency which I cannot yet place ... oh yes, didn't I mention it before? The Turkish people are amongst the friendliest, most hospitable types you could ever hope to meet.

Ten things you should know about Turkey

[Trip undertaken June 1989]

1. Currency is the Turkish lira (now, since 2005, it is the new Turkish lira which removed six zeroes from the previous lira).

2. Turks do not use sink plugs since Muslims believe it is offensive to wash in standing water. (They have no problem with swimming pools however.) Take a universal sink plug with you.

3. You cannot (as in Greece) put toilet paper down the loo. A small bin is provided. Shut your eyes and think of roses!

4. You won't find pork or bacon for sale since it's a Muslim country. Most Turks do seem to drink, however.

5. The national drink is chai (tea) usually served in small glasses, with loads of sugar. Delicious (but tell them if you don't want sugar added). Several varieties are available—apple, chamomile, sage, lemon, peppermint. The local firewater is *raki* (tastes like ouzo or Pernod).

6. Most Turks smoke and are football mad. Mention any footballer and you're likely to be hugged and kissed on both cheeks (if they like the one you've mentioned)!

7. The local tap water is not particularly poisonous but bottled water tastes nicer. The Turkish word for water is *su*.

8. English is not universally spoken even in some fairly touristy areas. German is widely spoken and you may fare better with a few *ja*'s and *nein*'s. In restaurants you can usually get by with pointing to items on display in the kitchen; this is even encouraged by the owners.

9. Tipping is usually done at a level of about 10%. Taxi drivers don't usually expect tips.

10. The most common mode of transport is the dolmus. They're ridiculously cheap, but can be uncomfortable for long journeys if you have to stand or crouch in them.

Further Reading

Turkey: A Travel Survival Kit by Tom Brosnahan (Lonely Planet Guides).
Istanbul and the Aegean Coast (Berlitz Travel Guide).
Turkish for Travellers (Berlitz).

Conclusions

Films, books, travel—this collation of my thoughts over three decades are, of course, only a smattering of the things I've experienced and enjoyed so far in life. True to say though, that what we read and what we see can influence not just what we *do* in the world, but what and how we *feel* about it. My travel articles for instance tend to be travel-filtered-through-film or art in many instances. A walk in Central Park, New York, brought forth memories of *Rosemary's Baby*, New Orleans—a reminder of A *Streetcar Named Desire*; Marigot Bay—a glimpse of *Doctor Dolittle*; Ölüdeniz—references to photographer and artist Ansel Adams and David Hockney, etc. Nothing is really forgotten by the brain but stored secretly away, available for cross-referencing if needed. Whether always relevant is another matter!

A camera will always record what you *see*; it will never record what you (or anyone else) *feel*. Criticism, whether on films, books, or travel, is essentially about how one *feels* as well as *what* one sees or reads.

I sometimes wonder why I've not written my memoirs to date. Now, in some ways, I think I already have.

Bibliography

1. imdb.com (International Movie Database). For details of cast and crew, plot summary, locations, goofs, trivia, trailers, audience reviews, and more, this is an invaluable online resource. Established online in 1993.

2. rottentomatoes.com. Collates published reviews of films and rates the percentage which are positive. Established in 1998 by three students from the University of California. It rather controversially converts a critic's score (conventionally 1–5 stars for a film) to a binary 'rotten' (negative) or 'fresh' (positive) score. Scores of four or five stars will be fresh; scores of one or two (and sometimes three) will be rotten. It's more useful to read the review than look at the score. One can filter results by All Critics or Top Critics, but this classification is also subjective!

3. Halliwell's *Who's Who in the Movies* (4th ed.) (Harper Collins; 2006).

4. Halliwell's *DVD Film and Video Guide* (1st ed.) (Harper Collins Entertainment; 2007).

5. *Production Design* by Fionnuala Hannigan (Ixel Books; 2012).

6. *Alfred Hitchcock: A Life in Darkness and Light* by Patrick McGilligan (Harper Collins; 2004).

7. *Cinematography* by Mike Goodridge and Tim Grierson (Ixel Books; 2012).

8. *For Keeps* by Pauline Kael (thirty years of collected reviews). (Penguin; 1996).

9. Artofthetitle.com (An online blog on title design and title sequences).

10. *Cinema Paradiso* screenplay by Giuseppe Tornatore (Faber and Faber; 1994).

11. *Hitchcock/Truffaut* by Francois Truffaut (Simon & Schuster; 1985). First published in 1966.

12. *A Snowdonia Childhood: A London Boy Growing Up in Beddgelert* by Richard J. Bernard (Gwasg Carreg Galch; 2013).

13. *Saul Bass: A Life in Film and Design* by Jennifer Bass and Pat Kirkham (Laurence King Publishing; 2011).

14. *Ever, Dirk: The Bogarde Letters* edited by John Coldstream (Weiden & Nicholson; 2003)

Diolch am ddarllen
Pob hwyl yn y sinema, a'r darllen a teithio.

Thanks for reading.
All the best with the cinemagoing, reading, and travel.

<u>Acknowledgment</u>

The author thanks Nigel Hughes, Porthmadog for assistance with the photographs.